Washable & Dryable Needlepoint

Washable & Dryable Needlepoint

Emily S. Sheldon

ARCO PUBLISHING, INC.
NEW YORK

Published by Arco Publishing, Inc.
219 Park Avenue South, New York, N. Y. 10003

Library of Congress Cataloging in Publication Data
Sheldon, Emily S.
　　Washable and dryable needlepoint.

　　1. Canvas embroidery.　I. Title.
TT778.C3S47　　　　746.44′2　　　　81−4667
ISBN 0−668−05174−4 (Cloth Edition)　　AACR2

Printed in the United States of America

Contents

Acknowledgments

In order to complete a project of this size, I have depended on many dedicated people. They were my samplemakers, models, "go-fers," draftsmen, teachers, and partisans. It is to all of these people that I dedicate this book with love:

Alicia Balda, Andy Benedicktus, Dana Benedicktus, Liz Benedicktus, Betsy Biggs, Peg Brennen, Helen Burtch, Marsha Cunningham, Edie Deal, Beth Dobbs, Mary Dobbs, Liz Kainz, Carol Kiplinger, Gail Kiplinger, Peter Kiplinger, Linda Kopetti, Alice Langenberg, Mary Kay Masterson, Mary Campbell McDonald, Barbara McDougal, Sally McDougal, Barbara McDowell, Lucy McReynolds, Pat O'Connell, Ilene Osherow, Ruthellen Osherow, Helen Payne, Mary Peterson, Mary Ruprecht, Jude Simmons, Lori Simmons, Victoria Simmons, Mary Beth Tinsley.

Also, many thanks to ESSence designs, ltd., Selwyn Hotchner, W. B. Kiplinger, and Harry Walters. Plus deep gratitude to Juliet Robinson and Natalie Sheets of the Webster Groves Bookshop.

Photography by Irvin Rader, with contributions from Frank Suits.

For editing and moral support I thank Pat Fisher, Olga Vezeris, and Virginia Griffin.

Introduction: "Designs On You"

If an introduction is to be taken literally, I should introduce myself: my name is Emily Simmons Sheldon and I am a free-lance designer. In 1976, in between working as an interior designer and restoring an old house on my own, I began researching ways of making needlepoint machine-washable and -dryable. This concept was a great challenge to me. Eventually, ESSence designs, ltd., was born and I have been happily designing and stitching ever since! Sharing my discoveries with you through this book has been a most exciting project.

All my life I have been a lover of the arts. I grew up in the antebellum atmosphere of my family's home in St. Louis, Missouri. As a child, I learned that some of our old paintings were done by my great-grandmother and the "reverse-glass" painted table tops had been painted by *her* aunt. The enchanting sampler that hung beside an old photo was worked by a child for her little sister in 1845. When I watched my grandfather working on his botanical drawings, and my mother needlepointing the insert for an antique tilt-top table, I simply took it for granted that all of these wonderful treasures were created by people just like us. I guess that is why I have never been shy about trying my hand at artistic projects.

The most important thing I learned about heirlooms was the joy of living with them and using them. I don't think I would enjoy living in a museum, and I must admit I am a "permanent press" person! However, my challenge has been to combine the best of these worlds.

Needlepoint has always been popular, but its evolution has been hampered by limited materials. It stands to reason, then, that the design scope was also restricted by the limited uses for the worked canvases.

Here we have a traditional craft just ripe for change. The sophistication of materials now offered in shops across our country indicates that we are ready to enjoy a 20th-century approach to needlework. We have new threads and yarns, canvases of every fiber and weave, permanent inks and paints, colors of many rainbows. But, most exciting of all, when we have needlepoint that can be worn and laundered, we have multiplied its usability and expanded the horizons of its design.

In closing, let me tell you (in case you haven't guessed): I've got "Designs on You"! I hope you enjoy them.

SECTION 1

Getting Started:
How to Use This Book

Welcome to the new world of machine-washable and -dryable needlepoint. On these pages you will find many new and exciting uses for a long revered and traditional craft. A glossary of terms containing both definitions and illustrations is included, so there should be no confusion between you—the novice or the experienced stitcher—and me.

The glossary includes basic stitch directions, finishing techniques and other general instructions. You will also discover that the stitch diagrams are for both right- and left-handed needleworkers. There is an appendix listing resources for products and finishing services. Items included in the appendix are marked throughout by an asterisk (*).

When selecting your project, be aware that many designs are from my "Designs-A-Foot" collection (these are marked DAF); they are easily interchangeable. Any of these designs would look great as a belt, a strap to wrap around a tote bag, or even a snappy pair of suspenders.

Hardware and notions resources can be found in the appendix. The alphabets and numerals included make it easy for you to personalize and date your projects. Don't forget to try the patches in a frame or several together as a pillow top. Be sure to calculate these changes when you organize your materials. The brand names given are for products I have used successfully in my research of this technique, and therefore I highly recommend them.

Materials

Permanent markers: Use Nepo™ and Glad Rags™ markers.* Combined they offer a broad color range.
Thread: DMC* 6-ply cotton embroidery floss.
Canvas: #12 interlock (exceptions are noted on projects).
Paint: tube of artist's white acrylic paint for corrections (do *not* use typing correction fluid).
Brush: artist's small paintbrush.

Technique

Pre-wash article to be decorated.

Test canvas by dipping the corner into a cup of boiling water; let dry. If all sizing washes out and the canvas is limp when dry, do not pre-wash. Otherwise, fold canvas and place it in a heat-proof glass container. Pour boiling water over it. After 10 minutes, remove and put in the dryer or air dry.

Measure the canvas on your article after washing and drying, as some canvas may shrink in the first washing.

---

* See Appendix

Transfer the design to the canvas. Use only the recommended markers since they will not bleed. Use only the white acrylic paint for corrections. Each pattern is in the most convenient place on the page for you to transcribe. If the pattern has many shades or colors, be prepared to change marker colors into a code. For example:

(A) dark green = blue marker
     medium green = green marker   or
     light green = yellow marker

(B) navy blue = black marker
     medium blue = blue marker
     light blue = green marker

The background is usually left blank. The background color is indicated by **BG** in the color key of each pattern. Try not to use a dark marker under a light-colored thread. Now you are ready to mark the centers of the canvas and the pattern. These are the reference points from which to begin. Remember that the pattern may be reduced or enlarged.

Thread: The term "thread" will be defined as a length of 6-ply embroidery floss. This amount includes a minimum overage of 15 percent. All thread counts are given in *skeins*.

Stitching: Never knot your thread on the back side. Either weave the ends into the back of the canvas or make a large knot and catch it on the face of the canvas beyond the design area. It may be cut off after several stitches have secured it.

Stitches: The most frequently used and recommended stitches are Continental and Basketweave. These and other special stitches used are defined and illustrated in the glossary.

Finishing: Illustrated instructions are given in the glossary as *Method A, B, or C.* Any special techniques will be described with the design.

SECTION 2

Glossary: Terms, Stitches and Finishing Techniques

Belts, suspenders, jumper/overall straps: To find the proper length for a belt that will be professionally finished with leather, measure your waist size over your clothing, then subtract 4 inches. Stitch this length, being sure to allow two extra border rows on the top and bottom that will be turned under. Stitch 2 full inches of perfectly plain background on each end. The remainder is the design area.

Belts, suspenders, and straps can be relatively easy and inexpensive to make. Careful measuring is an important step. If you are using a non-adjustable closure, use this formula: From the finished measurement, subtract the width or length of the clasp as it would be when worn. When you buy hardware that is adjustable, there will usually be instructions on the package. After finishing according to Method A, attach hardware and adjust to fit, then apply the backing.

Blocking: Blocking puts your canvas back to its original shape. Some canvases require only to be steam pressed and pinned down to the ironing board until dry. Whenever you do this, put a terry cloth over the face of the canvas and be careful not to apply pressure with the iron.

Assemble the following materials: brass or aluminum tacks or rustproof push-pins; a smooth flat surface of plywood or covered fiberboard large enough to be a comfortable work area; a drawing of lines spaced 1 inch apart in both directions to tack on the board, or draw the grid directly onto the board. This guide works equally well for round and square canvases.

Wet the canvas thoroughly, pat dry, and lay it on top of the grid face up. For square canvases, align one side and the top with an exact corner, then tack them down about 1 inch apart. Next, do the other side; do the bottom last. Oval and round canvases should be aligned on their bisecting centers. Remember that you can always remove a tack anytime for adjustments—you don't need to start over!

Tacking will make "holes" in your canvas, so I suggest tacking on or beyond the edge if possible. Some projects only respond to multiple pins right through the canvas and the holes can be worked out with steam, a working instrument (needle), and a bit of patience!

Method A: How to Finish an Edge on Interlock Canvas

The general rule is ½ inch for edges on small projects with up to 2 inches on larger ones. Pre-wash all possible materials.

Square canvas: (See Fig. 1.) Miter the corners to avoid extra thickness. (1) Cut corners in a rounded fashion, leaving at least ¼ inch of canvas right at the corner. (2) Turn under and tack down in the center. (3) Clip on each side close to the folds. (4) Refold and tack down on both sides.

Rounded canvas: (See Fig. 2.) (1) On circular or uneven edges, it is possible to clip right down to the stitching if you are careful. (2) Trim by angling the clipped canvas

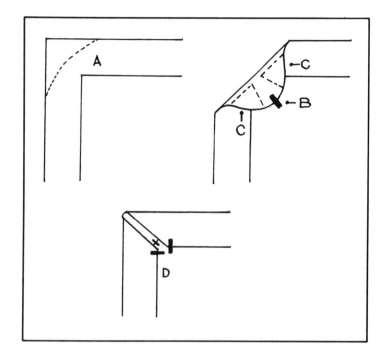

Fig. 1.   Method A—Square Canvas

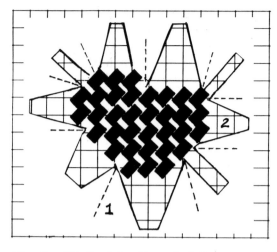

Fig. 2.   Method A—Rounded Canvas

and tack down. If this technique makes you nervous, stitch an outline like the shape of this example on scrap canvas and practice.

Stitching and Binding: I usually machine-stitch with "invisible" nylon thread to avoid changing colors constantly. (Now you know all my secrets!) A general weight sewing thread in a matching color is also fine for hand or machine sewing. When using the machine, stitch between the first and second rows of needlepoint on the edge. Figure out each of the possible steps needed to finish your project and make an outline something like this:

> miter corners; trim canvas and fold under; stitch down; add piping and stitch; add lace and stitch; stitch canvas to project; glue canvas to project.

Now see how many steps you can combine. For example: *Miter*—necessary; *trim and fold*—necessary; *piping, lace, and folded edge* can be stitched in one step with the help of a little pinning or basting; *apply to project* by hand or machine stitching or gluing. To glue your finished canvas to any item, apply Elmer's Glue-All™ moderately to the item to be decorated. Gently smooth out the canvas, then hold it firmly in place with masking tape or small tacks. Allow it to dry overnight.

Method B: Pillows and Projects with Similar Construction

Two rows of needlepoint will be lost on all seamed sides in the finishing process. Should this interfere with the design or size of your project, then stitch two additional rows where necessary.

Preshrink all materials. Measure and cut the fabric you will need with a ⅝-inch seam allowance including the back, the gusset, and/or the piping. Construct an inner pillow (optional) using the same method. Baste piping to front and back. With right sides facing each other, machine-stitch three sides and all four corners, being sure to round them off. Leave one side open.

Trim the seams in layers, cutting the needlepoint, if necessary, on the corners. Turn right side out and stuff with polyester fiber-fill, or use the optional inner pillow. Rounded, well-stuffed corners are the marks of a pro! Stitch the remaining seam and enjoy.

Method C: Picture Framing

If you choose to frame your canvas, you can either construct a custom frame or purchase pre-cut lengths of framing or ready-mades. The size of a frame is based on the back opening, but you must take into account the opening size. For example, if you buy two pairs of 10-inch lengths, you can fit a 10-by-10-inch mounted canvas into the back. However, the ¼-inch lip on all sides leaves you with an actual 9½-by-9½-inch design area.

Before you finish stitching the background, it is always a good idea to try the canvas taped to the mounting board in the frame. It is also attractive to mat your canvas, but please don't use glass—it ruins the texture of those beautiful stitches!

After blocking, place your canvas on the board and temporarily tack the edges. Make sure that the canvas is straight and that the lip covers what it is supposed to. When you are satisfied, pull the canvas margin around the edge and staple it to the back. Remove the tacks from the front and secure your needlepoint in its frame.

You can cover the back of the frame with paper; this is a perfect place to record the details of the canvas along with the full names of those involved and the appropriate dates. That way you will make future historians very happy!

Monogramming: On a sheet of any size graph paper, copy the stitches of your letters, using one dot for each stitch. Draw a line through the first row of empty grid on every side of the letters. Find the center in both directions within this area and mark with an **x**. From this point darken the same number of grid lines that would equal one inch of your canvas. Counting in reference to stitches, figure the equivalent of your maximum border. Now you can adjust the letters and spaces to fit your needs.

Refer to pp. 121–127 for the complete alphabets used in the projects shown here. (The final revisions of these alphabets may show a discrepancy in comparison with the photographs. In behalf of improvement, these changes seemed necessary.)

Splice: If you need to splice canvas together, lay one piece on top of another. Make sure to line them up evenly. Then paste or tape the pieces together and continue to stitch. This technique can also be used on DAFs to make them any length you wish.

Stitches: How To
Understand the Diagrams

Each basic stitch is formed by passing the thread across an intersection of canvas going *from bottom left mesh to top right mesh*. The numbers on both ends of the stitches in the illustration indicate the correct sequence of stitches. The odd numbers show the mesh where the needle is coming up from the back, and the even numbers show the mesh where the needle goes down into the back to complete the stitch.

Basketweave: This is the most valuable stitch to learn. Always try to use the Basketweave stitch for the background and as many other areas as you can. It can help alleviate distortion of the canvas. The Basketweave produces a very durable and wearable canvas. Begin in the upper right-hand corner. Left-handers, begin in the lower left-hand corner. (See Fig. 3.) Use a doubled thread.

Binding Stitch: This stitch is very useful for finishing a piece or for binding two pieces together. It's decorative, too. (See Fig. 4.) Use a doubled thread. Fold the canvas over, leaving one open row next to the stitching. Begin at the top right edge (or at the bottom left edge if you are left-handed). Take two anchor stitches, then go out over the edge, down four rows to B, and come in from behind. Go out over the edge again, come up two rows to C, and come in from behind. Repeat the same steps; from C go directly to A, and so forth. Begin and end threads as in stitching; keep the 4-2-4 pattern of stitches the same.

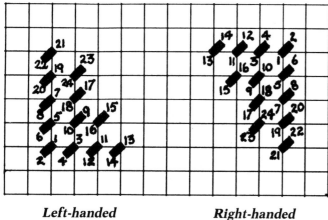

Left-handed   *Right-handed*

Fig. 3.   Basketweave

Fig. 4.   Binding Stitch

Brick II: (See Fig. 5.) Using a doubled strand, stitch this vertical pattern in a 6-2-6 repeat, alternating every other row as shown.

Buttonhole/Eyelet: (See Fig. 6.) Practice these stitches first and try them out for size. It is always best to do buttonhole/eyelets in the beginning of the project in order to have sufficient space in which to work.

Measure the length or size of the proposed buttonhole or eyelet, translate this figure into rows of holes, and mark the opening on the canvas. Use at least two rows in width for ease in opening.

Using half the amount of thread usually used, lay a border of supporting stitches, three or four rows in length, around the proposed opening. Next, stitch over the reinforcing threads. Use the same stitch as in the rest of the project, but again use only half the usual amount of thread.

After completing these steps, carefully cut away the center rows marked for the opening.

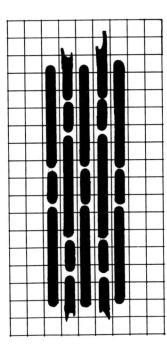

Fig. 5. Brick II

Alternating Verticals   *Scheme: 6–2–6*

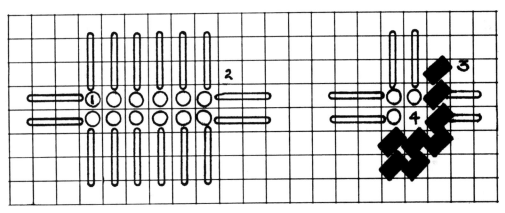

Fig. 6. Buttonhole/Eyelet

Continental: Use this stitch for small or "broken" areas not suited for the Basketweave stitch. (See Fig. 7.) Begin in the upper right-hand corner of the area. Left-handers, begin in the lower left-hand corner. Turn the canvas around at the end of the row and begin as before, stitching in the same direction. Use a doubled thread.

Eyelet: *See* Buttonhole/Eyelet.

French Knot: (See Figs. 8 and 9.) This stitch is the same as the embroidery stitch. Hold your needle in one hand and thread in the other. Wrap the thread around the needle in any one of the ways listed below. Pull the thread taut and hold while pushing the needle through to the back.

French Knots can be worked with a single or double thread; the thread may be wrapped once or twice around the needle. The French Knot is considered a regular stitch (Plaid Sampler) or a decorative stitch worked on top of a finished canvas (Bugs and Such).

French Knots vary a great deal with each stitcher. Where *you* might only need to work alternating stitches in the Plaid Sampler, I might stitch tightly and need to work

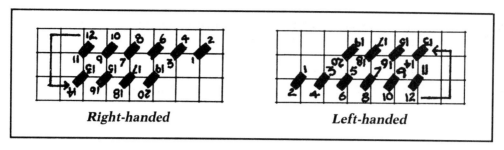

Fig. 7. Continental

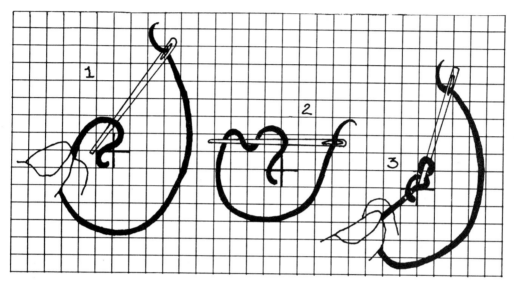

Fig. 8. French Knots

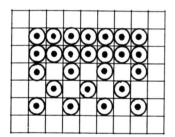

Fig. 9. French Knots

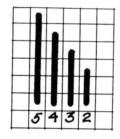

Fig. 10. Gobelin

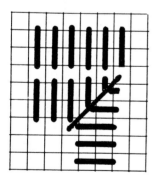

**Fig. 11. Gobelin—
Mitered Corner**

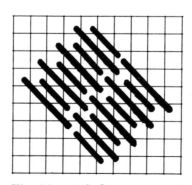

Fig. 12. Gobelin—Diagonal

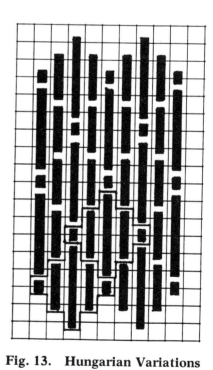

Fig. 13. Hungarian Variations

*Alternating Diamond Shapes
Scheme: 1–3–5–3–1*

12

every hole in order to cover the canvas. The best rule to follow is to do some practice stitches and decide what works best for you.

Gobelin: (See Fig. 10.) This stitch is worked horizontally or vertically. The number that usually follows the word *Gobelin* indicates the number of rows spanned per stitch. Be careful not to pull your stitches too tight or leave them too loose. There will be a noticeable crease where the rows of stitches meet, but do not worry as this is an acceptable characteristic of Gobelin. Figure 11 shows how to turn the corner. If a diagonal line crosses the corner, it indicates use of an overlay stitch that gives the mitered corner a finished look. Use a doubled thread.

Gobelin Diagonal: The same stitch as above, with the exception of its diagonal direction. (See Fig. 12.)

Hungarian Variation: (See Fig. 13.) This diamond-shaped pattern is a combination of vertical stitches in the scheme 1-3-5-3-1. The rows alternate to accommodate the diamond pattern. Use a doubled thread.

Overlay: A term used to indicate stitches that are added on top of a finished canvas. For example, the "Bugs and Such" design calls for a simple stitch to represent the bugs' antennae. In case a full thread is too much, separate the thread and use only 2- or 3-ply. These stitches are merely decorative and there are really no right or wrong stitches.

An Overlay stitch is a good finishing touch when laid over the mitered corner in the Gobelin stitch. (See Gobelin stitch illustrations.)

Rice Stitch: (See Fig. 14.) The primary stitch is a large diagonal **X** that measures 5 holes each way. Complete these, then add 4 smaller stitches, 3 holes in length diagonally. Cross the main stitch on each of its four ends, forming a diamond shape and overlapping the large crosses. Use a doubled strand.

Stepping Stitch: (See Fig. 15.) First use the Continental stitch to define the areas marked ♦ in a pattern of 5 up and 5 over. Fill in with a diagonal Gobelin stitch. Use a doubled thread.

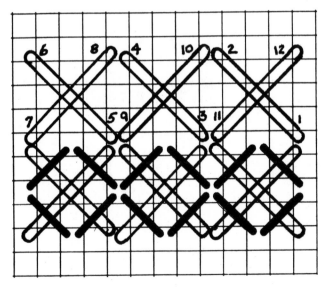

Fig. 14.   Rice Stitch
First Step, Large Cross: 5 × 5 diagonal
Second Step, Four-Diamond Shape

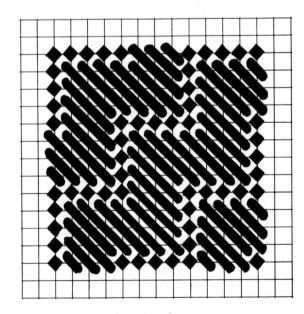

Fig. 15.   Stepping Stitch
Continental Stitch
Gobelin/Diagonal

Tweed: This effect is obtained by stitching with two colors that are worked together. Thread one strand of each color into your needle and stitch as usual. The result looks "tweedy."

Woven Bands: (See Fig. 16.) (A) Lay a doubled strand across the area to be covered, making sure it is on a true diagonal. Lay the rest of the thread in the same direction, using every other row. Be cautious about keeping the tension too tight. (B) Use another thread to work the opposite diagonals coming up in the alternate holes. (C) Take the needle and actually weave in and out of the opposite threads that are laid on top of the canvas. After stitching down, come up in the next open space and continue weaving.

    Recommendation: After completing each thread, change direction in order to tack down the long loose threads of the first step.

Zigzag Stitch: (See Fig. 17.) This stitch is used when two ends of a finished canvas are butted together just after being glued down on a hard surface. It is generally just a precautionary step, but I feel better after using it! Use a sewing needle and thread to catch the canvas ends.

W-D (Washable and Dryable): Every item made with the recommended materials is machine-washable and -dryable, provided of course that the items they are applied to or finished with are also W-D. Washable projects that are applied to items that can sustain only a temporary bath, such as wood, plastic, glass, or wool, can be gently scrubbed with a mild detergent using a baby's soft toothbrush.

    Because DMC uses ecologically safe dyes in accordance with federal standards, a minute amount of bleeding may occur, but it will disappear after the initial washing.

    Once you discover how practical and easy to care for washable and dryable needlepoint is, you will discover hundreds of new ways to decorate your world with needlepoint.

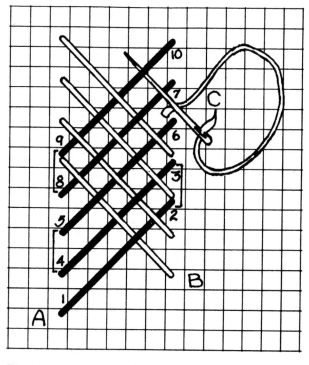

Fig. 16. Woven Bands

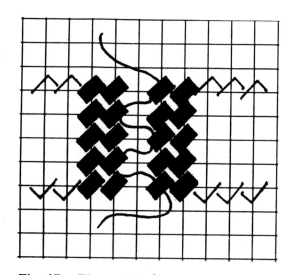

Fig. 17. Zigzag Stitch

SECTION 3

Patches

Strawberry Patch

A strawberry patch is a delightful addition to so many projects. It's a favorite design of Lori's and mine.

Materials: #12 interlock canvas, 5½″ by 5½″
(design area, 3½″ by 3½″)
½ yd. polyester eyelet lace

Color Key and Thread Count

Key	Color	Skeins	Key	Color	Skeins
⊡	666 Red	1	C	726 Yellow	1
B	602 Pink	1	O	White	1
A	701 Medium green	1	⊠	310 Black	1
●	909 Dark green	1	BG	704 Light green	3

Stitches: Continental, Basketweave

Finishing: Use Method A and work in eyelet lace. General.

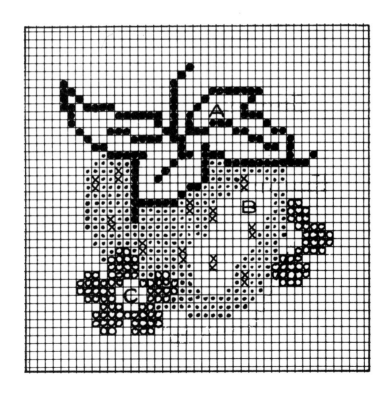

Model "A"

Who says a young man has to be sixteen to have his own car? Jude is very proud of his patch. I just wish he'd stop asking me if that's the kind of car I learned to drive in.

Materials: #12 interlock canvas, 5¾" by 5"
(design area, 3¾" by 3")
½ yd. binding

Color Key and Thread Count

Key	Color	Skeins	Key	Color	Skeins
⊡	701 Green	1	◼	310 Black	1
◻	498 Dark red	1	**BG**	White	3
⊠	414 Gray	1			

Stitches: Continental, Basketweave

Finishing: Use Method A.

18

Gingham Dog and Calico Cat

Now that he's so easy to care for, you can stitch this winsome pup for a patch pocket like Beth's—and don't forget his best friend!

Materials: #12 interlock canvas, two pieces 5½″ by 6″, each
(design area, 3½″ by 4″, each)

Color Key and Thread Count

	Key	Color		Skeins	Key		Color	Skeins
Dog	⊡	799	Light blue	1	⊿	666	Red	1
	⊿	797	Medium blue	1	Ⓐ		White	1
	◼	820	Dark blue	1	**BG**	906	Green	4
Cat	◼	498	Deep red	1	Ⓑ	818	Light pink	1
	⊡	309	Dark red	1	**BG**	906	Green	4
	Ⓐ	899	Dark pink	1					

Stitches: Continental, Basketweave

Finishing: Use Method A; add a backing for pocket.

Zinny

This is an adaptation from the zinnia, one of my very favorite summer flowers. The extravagant colors are true to this little beauty.

Materials: #12 interlock canvas, 6½″ by 6½″
(design area, 4½″ by 4½″)
⅔ yd. binding

Color Key and Thread Count

Key	Color	Skeins	Key	Color	Skeins
◨	307 Yellow	1	☐	552 Purple	1
▨	740 Orange	1	⊠	699 Dark green	1
▣	602 Pink	1	**BG**	704 Light green	5
⊡	321 Red	1			

Stitches: Continental, Basketweave

Finishing: Use Method A.

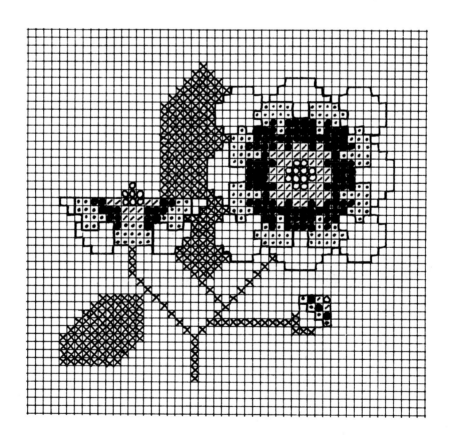

Geometry in Color

I'll have to give the rainbow credit for this color scheme, but I added the design. Together, they are certainly a handsome combination.

Materials: #12 interlock canvas, 7¼″ by 7¼″
(design area, 5¼″ by 5¼″)
¾ yd. binding

Color Key and Thread Count

Key		Color	Skeins	Key		Color	Skeins
⊡	666	Red	1	●	797	Blue	1
⊟	947	Orange	1	⊠	552	Purple	1
◨	307	Yellow	1	BG	809	Steel blue	6
◿	701	Green	1				

Stitches: Continental, Basketweave

Finishing: Use Method A.

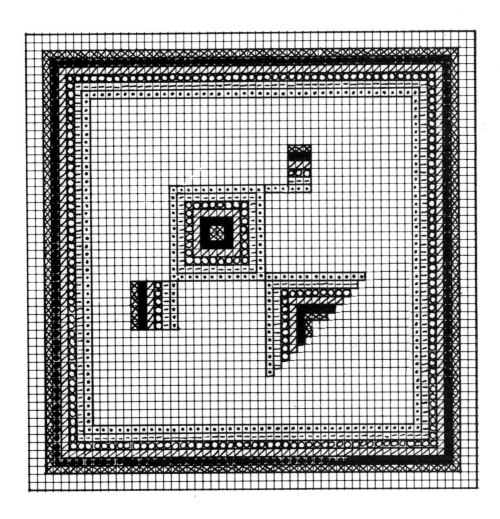

Peppermint Dip

Nobody can resist an ice cream cone—this one included. Those big chunks of peppermint look good enough to eat!

Materials: #12 interlock canvas, 5½" by 6½"
(design area, 3¼" by 4½")
½ yd. binding

Color Key and Thread Count

Key		Color	Skeins
⊡	604	Light pink	1
◨	601	Dark pink	1
☐	433	Brown	1
◻	436	Tan	1
BG	907	Green	3

Stitches: Continental, Basketweave, French Knot (peppermint bits)

Finishing: Use Method A.

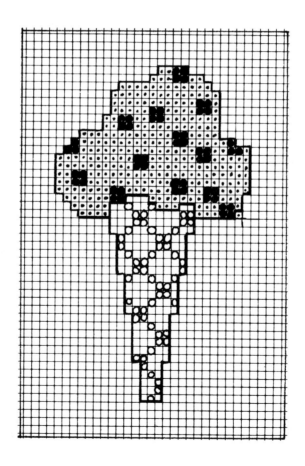

Patchwork Monogram

This "mini-sampler" is extremely popular. The center monogram makes it very special for the owner!

Materials: #12 interlock canvas, 6¼″ by 6″
(design area, 4¼″ by 4″)
⅔ yd. binding

Color Key and Thread Count

Key	Color	Skeins	Key	Color	Skeins
◘	666 Red	2	⊡	701 Green	1
⊠	947 Orange	1	◼	797 Blue	1
⊟	307 Yellow	1	**BG**	White	2

Special Instructions: Monogramming (see Glossary)

Stitches: Continental, Basketweave

Finishing: Use Method A.

Ball 'n' the Jacks

A simple game and a simple design, but the graphics are eye-catching.

Materials: #12 interlock canvas, 5½" by 5½"
(design area, 3½" by 3½")
½ yd. binding)

Color Key and Thread Count

Key	Color	Skeins
⊡	666 Red	2
◻	310 Black	1
BG	White	3

Stitches: Continental, Basketweave

Finishing: Use Method A.

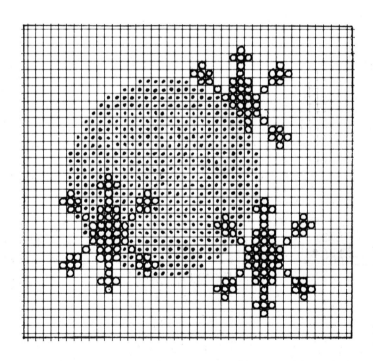

First Aid

No one needs a skinned knee or sore bottom for an excuse to wear these bandages. Make as many as you like and give them as gifts.

Materials: #12 interlock canvas, 6½″ by 6½″
(design area, 4½″ by 4½″)
⅔ yd. binding

Color Key and Thread Count

Key	Color	Skeins	Key	Color	Skeins
■	351 Dark pink	1	◨	712 Ecru	1
□	353 Light pink	2	**BG**	820 Navy	4

Stitches: Continental, Basketweave

Finishing: Use Method A.

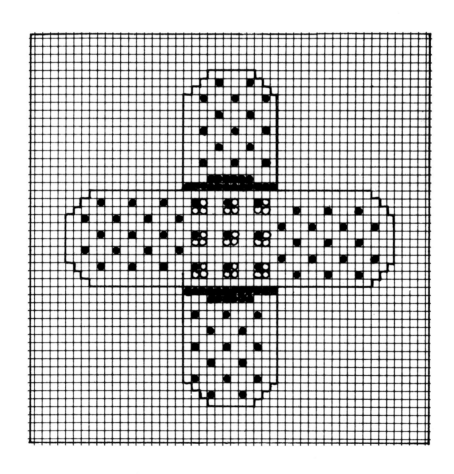

Free Wheelin'

Biking is more popular than ever. Even though this design shows a three-wheeler, I'll bet it appeals to everybody—even the ten-speeders.

Materials: #12 interlock canvas, 6½″ by 5¾″
(design area, 4½″ by 3¾″)
⅔ yd. binding

Color Key and Thread Count

Key	Color	Skeins	Key	Color	Skeins
▢	666 Red	1	⊡	317 Gray	1
⊠	797 Blue	1	**BG**	307 Yellow	5
◼	310 Black	1			

Stitches: Continental, Basketweave

Finishing: Use Method A.

Ship Ahoy

Even a landlubber will like this design. Who hasn't dreamed of being a ship's captain and sailing across the sea in pursuit of far-off treasures?

Materials: #12 interlock canvas, 5¼" by 5½"
(design area, 3¼" by 3½")
½ yd. binding

Color Key and Thread Count

Key	Color	Skeins
☐	White	1
◱	666 Red	1
◓	820 Navy	1
⊡	797 Blue	1
BG	809 Sky Blue	3

Stitches: Continental, Basketweave

Finishing: Use Method A.

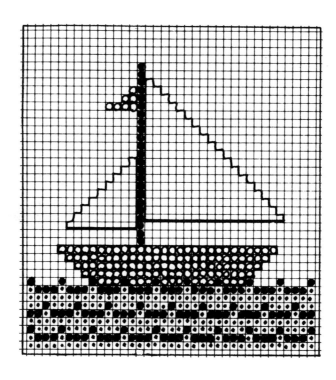

Hoss

This patch is dedicated to all of America's superheroes who rode the West and saved us all from the "bad guys."

Materials: #12 interlock canvas, 6¼" by 5¼"
(design area, 4¼" by 3¼")
⅔ yd. binding

Color Key and Thread Count

Key	Color	Skeins	Key	Color	Skeins
⊠	797 Dark blue	1	⊡	666 Light red	2
◼	310 Black	1	◘	498 Dark red	1
☑	972 Dark orange	1	**BG**	809 Light blue	3

Stitches: Continental, Basketweave

Finishing: Use Method A.

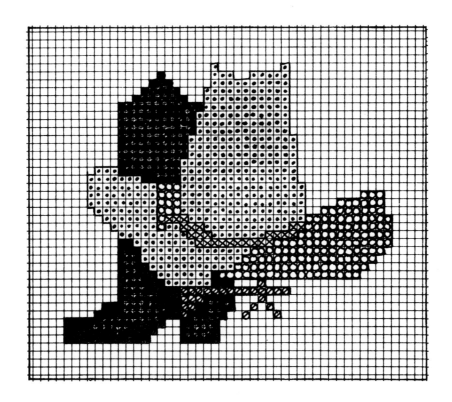

Magic Cubes

This geometric design was inspired by the old-fashioned "baby blocks" quilt pattern. The bold color scheme makes it perfect for today's fashions.

Materials: #12 interlock canvas, 6″ by 5¼″
(design area, 4″ by 3¼″)
⅔ yd. binding

Color Key and Thread Count

Key	Color		Skeins	Key	Color		Skeins
⊡	666	Red	1	⊘	701	Green	1
⊟	947	Orange	1	⊠	552	Purple	1
▣	307	Yellow	1	**BG**		White	2
▨	797	Blue	1				

Stitches: Continental, Basketweave

Finishing: Use Method A.

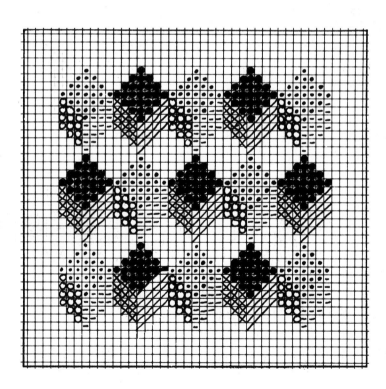

Teacher's Pet

Who wouldn't be swayed by these good-looking apples? It will be a favorite of both teachers and students.

Materials: #12 interlock canvas, 6½″ by 6½″
(design area, 4½″ by 4½″)
⅔ yd. binding

Color Key and Thread Count

Key	Color	Skeins	Key	Color	Skeins
⊡	666 Red	2	◙	434 Brown	1
⊠	947 Orange	1	☐	White	1
⊘	701 Green	1	**BG**	307 Yellow	4

Stitches: Continental, Basketweave

Finishing: Use Method A.

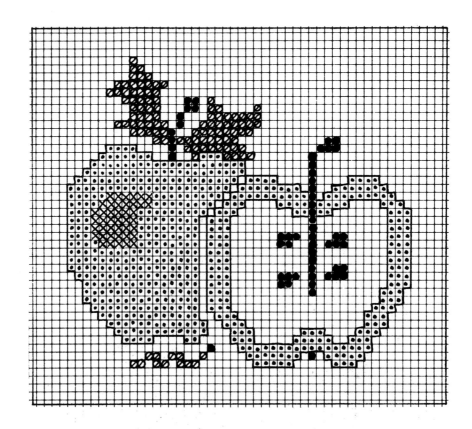

SECTION 4

Pillows

Fantasy Forest

This design is very lively and contemporary even though its inspiration is the old needle art of appliqué.

Materials: #12 interlock canvas, 18″ by 18″
(design area, 14″ by 14″)
½ yd. fabric for backing and piping
polyester fiber-fill

Color Key and Thread Count

Key	Color	Skeins	Key	Color	Skeins
1	909 Dark green	7	9	307 Yellow	6
2	701 Medium green	20	10	666 Red	2
3	704 Light green	5	11	947 Orange	5
4	798 Dark blue	3	12	740 Peach	2
5	809 Light blue	10	13	917 Magenta	2
6	433 Brown	2	14	603 Light magenta	2
7	920 Rust	2	BG	White	22
8	436 Camel	2			

Stitches: Continental, Basketweave

Finishing: Use Method B.

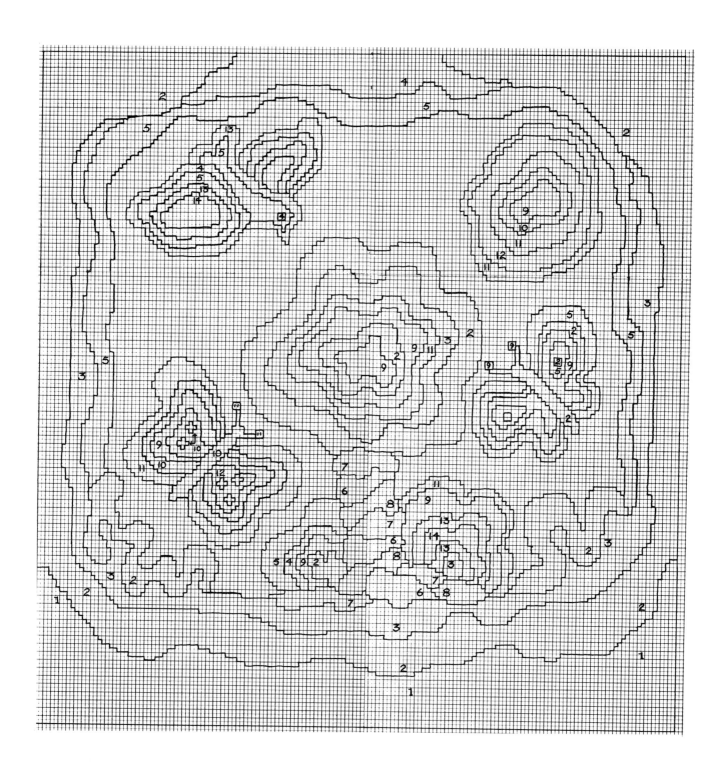

Quilt Lily

This lily design was adapted from several old quilt patterns. It has always been a favorite, and this version is as timeless and versatile as its predecessors.

Materials: #12 interlock canvas, 16″ by 16″
(design area, 12″ by 12″)
½ yd. fabric for backing and piping
polyester fiber-fill

Color Key and Thread Count

Square	Key		Color	Skeins	Square	Key		Color	Skeins
A	⊡	894	Light pink	1	F	⊡	794	Light larkspur	1
	⊠	892	Dark pink	1		⊠	792	Dark larkspur	1
B	⊡	799	Light iris	1	G	⊡	353	Light peach	1
	⊠	797	Dark iris	1		⊠	351	Dark peach	1
C	⊡	922	Light coral	1	H	⊡	519	Light peacock	1
	⊠	919	Dark coral	1		⊠	517	Dark peacock	1
D	⊡	993	Light dragonfly	1	I	⊡	726	Light day lily	1
	⊠	991	Dark dragonfly	1		⊠	783	Dark day lily	1
E	⊡	3688	Light rose	1	J	◻	907	Light green	20
	⊠	3685	Dark rose	1	K	◼	905	Dark green	18
					L and **BG**			White	25

Stitches: Continental, Basketweave, and Gobelin 4 (borders L, J, & K)

Finishing: Use Method B.

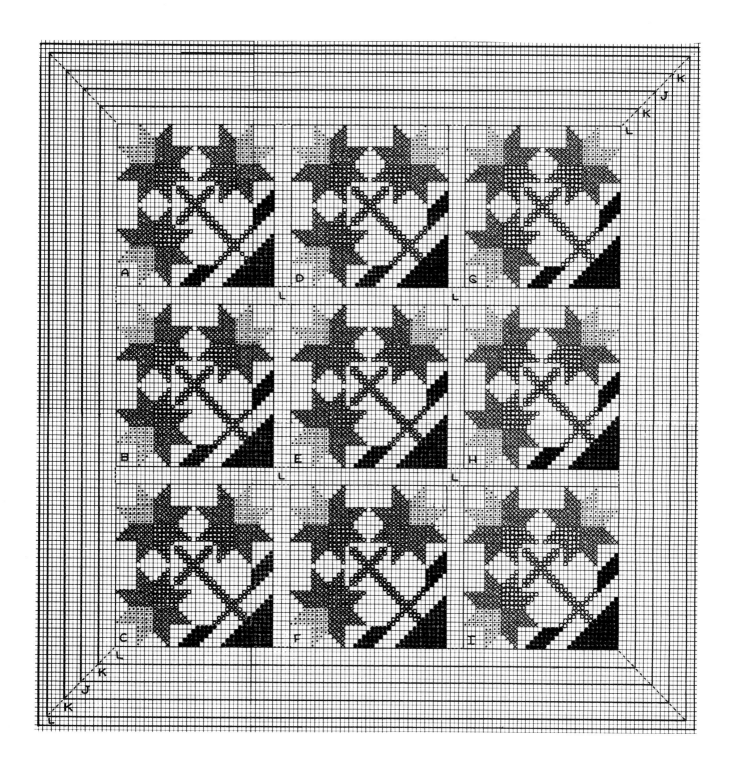

Decisions, Decisions

This pillow is not only divinely decorative, but it is totally functional (yes, the arrow really spins). Whether you are making corporate policy or deciding whom to invite to the prom, it will be fun to make Decisions, Decisions.

Materials: #12 interlock canvas, 14″ by 14″
(design area, 10″ by 10″ by 14″)
½ yd. fabric for backing and piping
one smooth "craft" bead no wider than the arrow, nor thicker than ¼″ (two thin beads may be stacked)
12″ of medium-weight nylon line (fishing line)

Color Key and Thread Count

Key	Color	Skeins
■	820 Navy	8
◪	307 Yellow	7
■	666 Red	3
◨	701 Green	6

Stitches: Continental, Basketweave

Finishing: Use Method B for the pillow. Use Method A for uneven canvases for the arrow. Attach the finished arrow before the pillow is constructed. Thread the nylon line and secure it to the arrow back. Thread the bead, then go through the center of the navy boundary lines and secure to the back of the canvas.

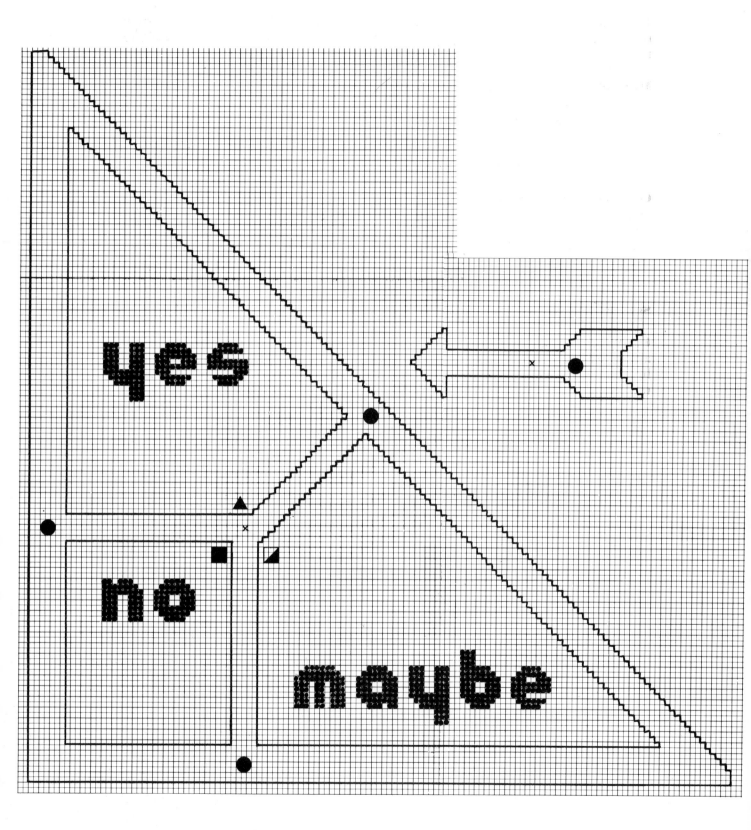

Cozy Kitty

This mini-pillow can curl up and be hugged or it can sit politely and wait for your affection. The striped gusset provides plenty of room to personalize it for someone special. It's a delight to stitch and is very easy to care for.

Materials: #12 interlock canvas, 11½" by 7" (face)
28" by 4" (gusset)
(design area, 8½" by 4½") (face)
25¼" by 1¾" (gusset)
½ yd. fabric for backing and piping
polyester fiber-fill

Color Key and Thread Count

Key		Color	Skeins
◙	797	Dark blue	5
B	809	Light blue	10
O	701	Green	3
Y	307	Yellow	8
O	970	Orange	6

◙   (to indicate where the stripes will match up when finished)

Special Instructions: The gusset is one long piece designed so that the colors will match up with the pillow front when they are sewn together. To stitch the gusset, start with Blue in the lower right-hand corner of the chart and continue, working counter-clockwise. I suggest that your stitch direction on the gusset be the same as on the pillow front, but only for the sake of beauty. Choose the most comfortable for you. Plot the name you want on a piece of graph paper. (See page 121 for monograms.) Center it anywhere on the gusset. Your initials and the date can also be stitched in with a smaller alphabet.

Stitches: Continental, Basketweave

Finishing: Use Method B. In order to align the stripes on the face and gusset, you should first baste by hand.

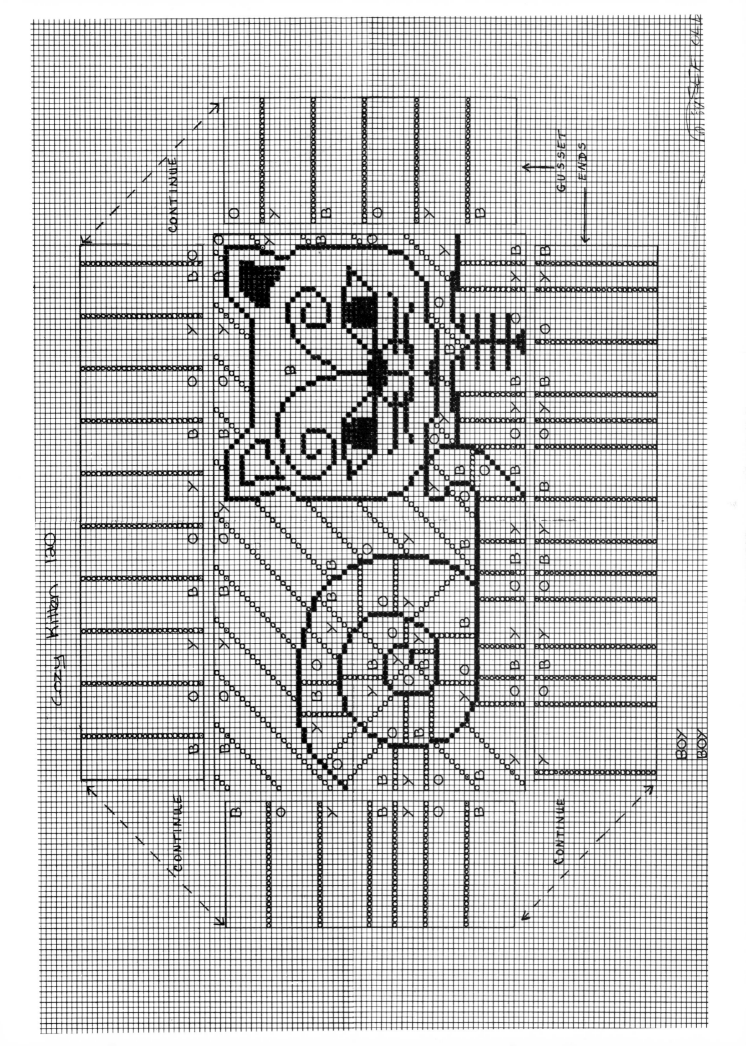

SECTION 5

Pictures

Dieter's Motto

If you are going to diet, you might as well enjoy it. This is one of the most "giveable" projects I know of. It will certainly give your laugh muscles a great workout.

Materials: #12 interlock canvas, 13″ by 10½″
(design area, 10″ by 7½″)
picture frame

Color Key and Thread Count

Key	Color	Skeins	Key	Color	Skeins
⊡	353 Light pink	5	▨	307 Yellow	1
■	351 Dark pink	3	⊠	799 Blue	1
⊡	701 Medium green	3	**BG**	White	18
⊟	909 Dark green	3			

Stitches: Continental, Basketweave, French Knot (pig's eyes and flower centers)

Finishing: Use Method C.

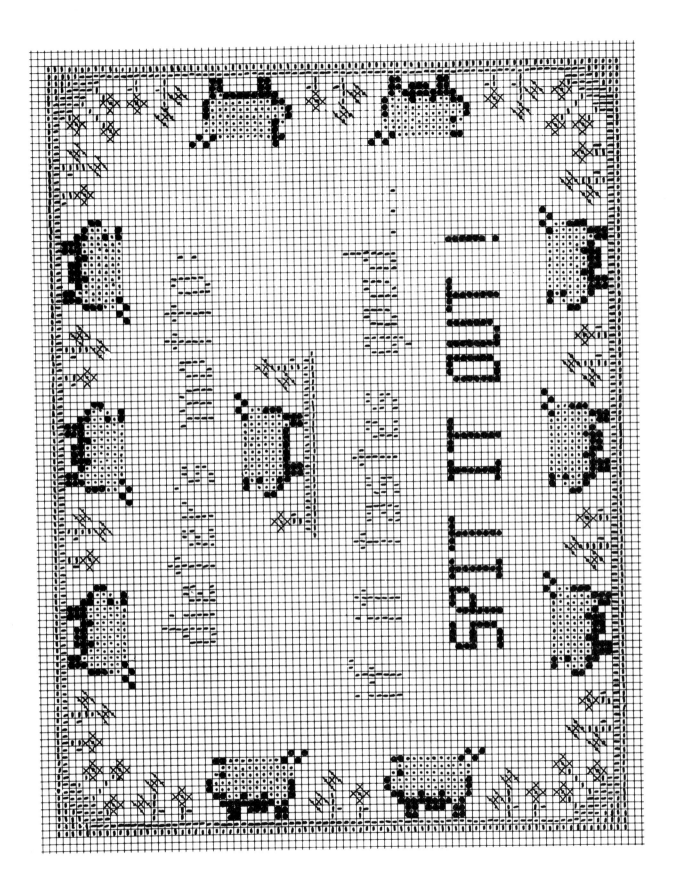

Rainbo on the Square

Each quadrant is a unique but integral part of this design. When the four sections are hung together, they offer a structured effect; the geometric shape of the background, as well as the "Rainbo," is handsomely distinct.

Materials: #12 interlock canvas, 26″ by 26″, made of 4 pieces 13″ by 13″
(design area, four pieces 9″ by 9″)
framing or fabric for finishing

Color Key and Thread Count

Key	Color	Skeins	Key	Color	Skeins
⊠	553 Purple	4	⊟	740 Orange	4
◼	799 Blue	4	⊡	891 Red	5
◿	703 Green	4	**BG**	712 Ecru	46
◻	726 Yellow	4			

Special Instructions: *Important:* Mark the entire design on the canvas before cutting it into quadrants. This insures a matched set of canvases and makes it easier to draw the design. The illustrations are both instructions and pattern. Follow the sequence of colors given in the color key above when stitching. (A) Mark quadrants off equally. Number each quadrant. (B) Find the centers of the dividing lines between the quadrants, marked as ⊕ on the pattern. (C) One "row" on this chart equals 5 stitches. Mark off 11 rows in each direction. Complete the square, which is 22 rows on all sides. Mark this design area on the three other quadrants. (D) Beginning in quadrant 1, first chart the pattern of the inner row (purple) marked X, then follow with the other 5 color symbols. (E) Plot the background rows as well, then draw all the rows in every section. Note mitered and butted corners—samples of each are given in quadrant 1 of pattern (See Fig. 18). One extra row all around is included in the design area to accommodate a frame or allow for pillow seams.

Stitches: Gobelin 5 and Gobelin 3, and use
Overlay on top of mitered corners.

Finishing: Use Method C.

Fig. 18. Rainbo on the Square

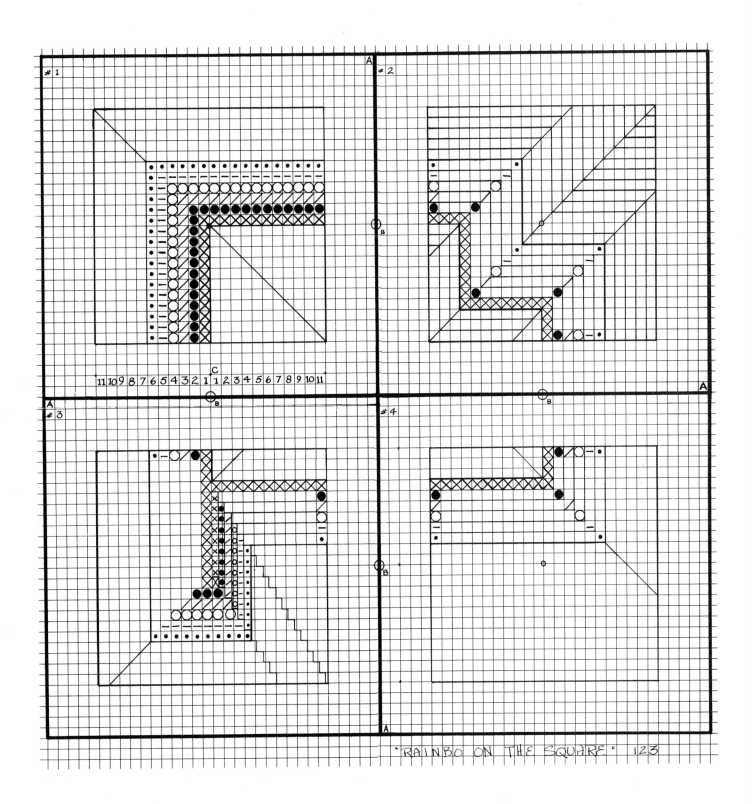

"RAINBO ON THE SQUARE" 123

Plaid Sampler

This contemporary sampler utilizes 6 different stitches in 18 very attractively combined colors. A rustic frame is only one of many choices—you might also try a sleek, thin chrome or a high-gloss white.

Materials: #12 interlock canvas, 16″ by 22″
(design area, 12″ by 18″)
picture frame

Color Key and Thread Count

Key	Color		Skeins	Key	Color		Skeins
1	809	Sky blue	4	10	907	Lime	3
2	518	Peacock	3	11	701	Kelly	4
3	820	Sea blue	4	12	943	Turquoise	3
4	517	Teal	3	13	904	Moss	3
5	3685	Burgundy	3	14	895	Hunter	3
6	744	Pale Yellow	1	15	434	Saddle	4
7	726	Buttercup	2	16	350	Bittersweet	4
8	742	Harvest	4	17	919	Russet	8
9	519	Robin's egg blue	5	18	823	Navy	4

Stitches:

Stitch	Color number
Rice	1, 11, 17
Woven Bands	5, 10, 14
French Knot	8, 9, 12
Brick II	6, 7, 15
Stepping Stitch	3, 16, 18
Hungarian Variation	2, 4, 13

Finishing: Use Method C.

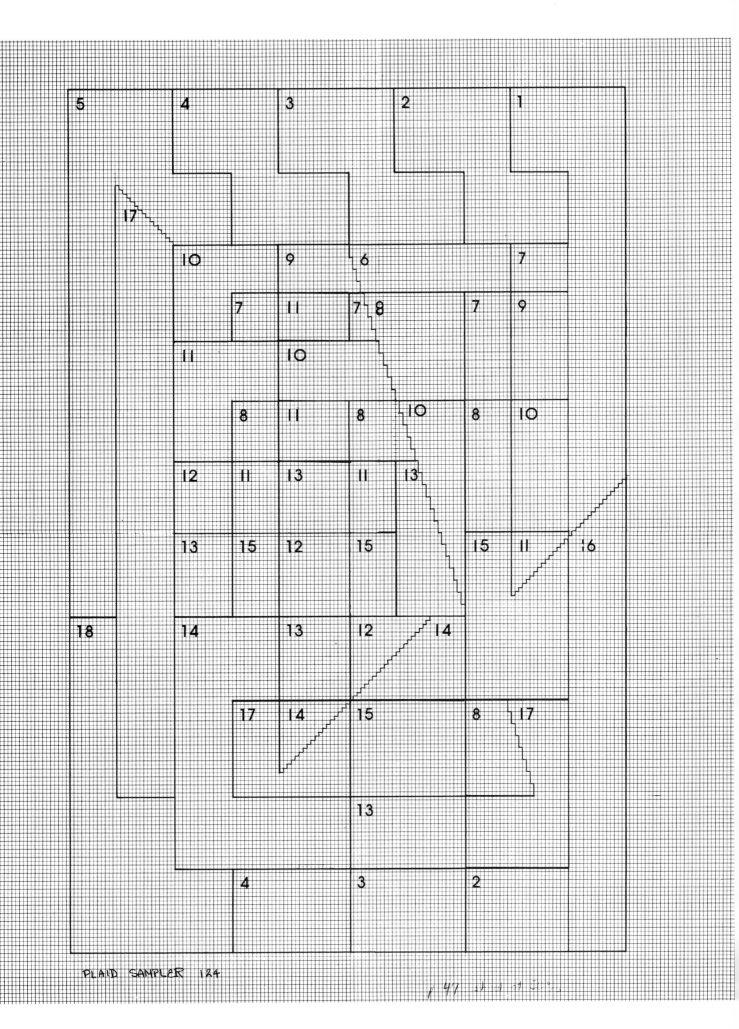

PLAID SAMPLER 124

I'm OK & You're OK

The title speaks for itself. Give this message to that "super" someone. Whether you choose to frame it or stuff it, there will always be a perfect place for this communication!

Materials: #12 interlock canvas, 18″ by 18″
(design area, 14″ by 14″)
picture frame

Color Key and Thread Count

Key	Color	Skeins
⊡	350 Coral	5
▨	704 Light green	10
▢	701 Medium green	10
⊠	909 Dark green	10
◧	797 Blue	9
BG	726 Yellow	42

Stitches: Continental, Basketweave

Finishing: Use Method C.

i'm OK & OK you're and together... we're SUPER!!!

Sweet Raspberries

A lovely design as a picture, or on a tote, or as the center of a pillow surrounded with ruffles. Enjoy this on whatever you choose.

Materials: #12 interlock canvas, 6″ by 6¼″
(design area, 4″ by 4¼″)
25½″ grosgrain ribbon
6″ by 6″ frame

Color Key and Thread Count

Key		Color	Skeins
⊠	309	Raspberry	1
◻	899	Pink	1
◉	726	Yellow	1
◼	909	Dark green	2
▨	703	Medium green	1
⊡	907	Light green	1
BG		White	4

Stitches: Continental, Basketweave, and French Knot (yellow)

Finishing: Use Method C.

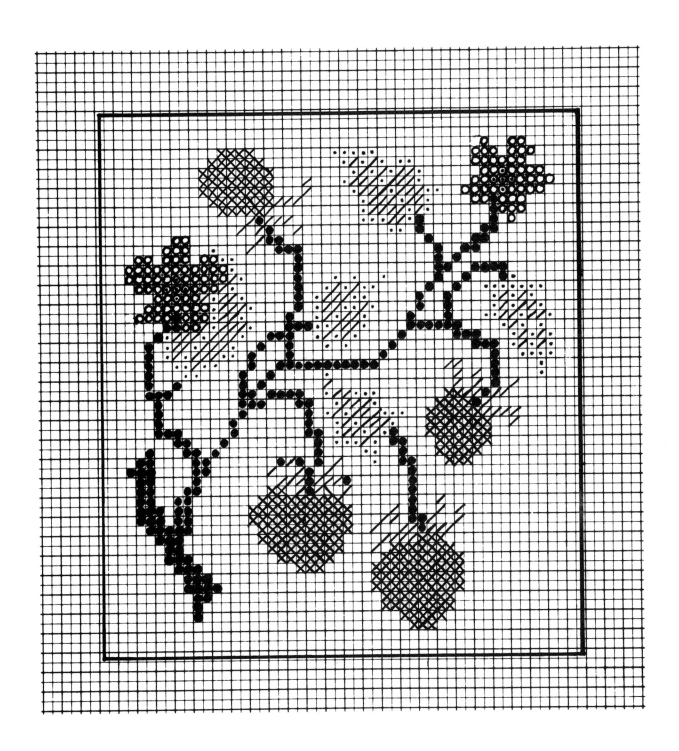

Sweet Violets

Nothing is a sweeter reminder of the gentle days of spring than these wonderful violets. You can frame them as you see here by following the coordinated instructions for the next pattern, Woven Bands Frame.

Materials: #12 interlock canvas, if framed, 9½" by 9½"; if unframed, 6" by 6¼" (design area, if framed, 6½" by 6½"; if unframed, 4" by 4¼")

Color Key and Thread Count

Key	Color	Skeins	Key	Color	Skeins
⊡	704 Light·green	1	◘	554 Lavender	1
⊘	701 Medium green	2	⊡	726 Yellow	1
◼	699 Dark green	2	**BG**	White	3
⊠	552 Purple	1			

Stitches: Continental, Basketweave, French Knot (yellow), and Overlay (petals)

Finishing: Use Method A. See finishing instructions for Woven Bands Frame, for framed version.

Woven Bands Frame

This charming design is a wonderful way to frame needlepoint. It's also perfect for photographs, because elaborate frames often detract from the picture. You can work this design on the same canvas you are framing, as we have done, or you can make it separately, as a project of its own.

Materials: #12 interlock canvas, 9½" by 9½"
(design area, 6½" by 6½")
¼" plywood, 6" by 6"
48" piece narrow ribbon
one piece of felt, 6" by 6"

Color Key and Thread Count

Key		Color	Skeins
◨	⊡	704 Light green	5
◪	◼	701 Dark green	8

Special Instructions: See Woven Bands (p. 14). When stitching the frame around a worked canvas, begin in the same holes as were used in the background of the project. To add this frame to a needlepoint project that does not have a canvas border large enough, see Splice (p. 9). To work as a frame only, use the same materials to make a 12-row-wide frame.

Stitches: Continental, Basketweave, Woven Bands

Finishing: To make the frame alone, add one row of Continental Stitch to all edges, inside and out. Use the finished Woven Bands as a pattern for the ¼-inch plywood. Cut the narrow ribbon into pieces that are one inch long on all sides. Stitch the ribbon between the row of Continental Stitch and the Woven Bands. Clip the inside and outside corners of the extra canvas. Stretch the canvas over the plywood frame and tack into place. Fold and handstitch the ribbons together at the corners; finish with a felt backing.

The Basketweave Triangle

I have heard aspiring needlepointers express strong doubts about learning the Basketweave stitch. I also have seen kids have a world of fun stitching, so I asked my friend Liz and her two children to help me see if we could do a project that was both fun and instructive. The results are pictured on Color Page 3. Andy, age six, opted for designing his own motif as well as his own stitches. Dana, age nine, chose a strawberry; she used the Continental stitch, which she mastered in a very short time. We dispensed with backgrounds for the kids, and gave their mom an assignment in that "difficult stitch."

The key to learning Basketweave lies in practice, because few designs employ the basic triangle used to demonstrate the stitch. Here I used that very triangle to create a simple frame for the strawberry. Liz was delighted to find the Basketweave stitch very comfortable after this brief exercise. She and her children have created future heirlooms and had a wonderful time in the process. (For stitching instructions, see *Basketweave* in the glossary.)

To determine the pattern, we measured the opening needed for the frame and rounded off our figures so that both dimensions were divisible by the number 8—32 stitches high by 40 stitches wide. By increasing or decreasing these dimensions and keeping them divisible by 8, you can vary the frame size to suit your particular projects.

Strawberry Patch and Model "A"

Hors d'Oeuvres on Parade and The Big Carrot

**Geometry in Color, Zinny, Patchwork Monogram,
Peppermint Dip, Ball 'n' the Jacks**

Asparagus Bouquet and Artichoke Rose

Fantasy Forest

Decisions, Decisions

Cozy Kitty

Quilt Lily

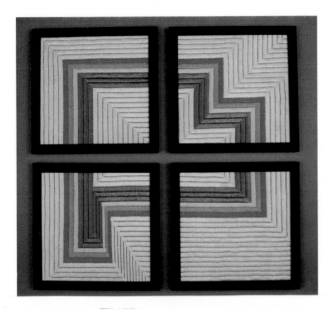

Rainbo on the Square

Dieter's Motto

Sweet Raspberries, Sweet Violets and Woven Bands Frame

Plaid Sampler

I'm OK & You're OK

Children's Projects showing Basketweave Triangle Frame

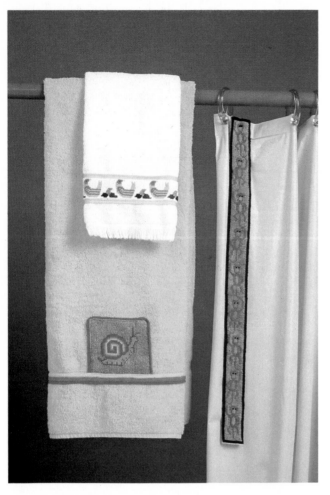

South on the Border, Snail's Pace and Monkey Business

Jogging Turtles and Butterflies are Free

Lily and the Frog

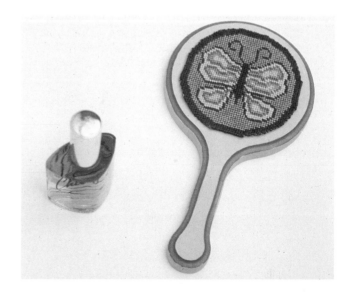

Butterfly Looking Glass

Rosebud Ribbon

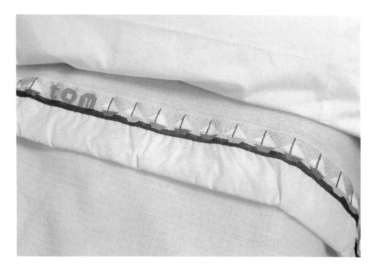

Sailor's Delight

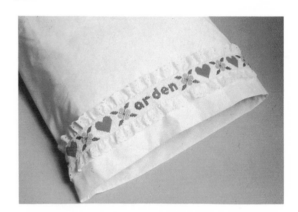

Hearts and Flowers

Garden Border

Rosebud Monogram

Bugs and Such

El Placebo

Walking Tall and Egyptian Eye

Afriqué

The Mouse Takes the Cheese

The World's Greatest

Backgammon Graphics

Sunshine and What's Your Game

On the Green

Grass Roots

Pups' and Kitties' Flea Collar

Christmas Tree Ornaments

Pot o' Gold

Gumballs Galore

Birds and Berries Holiday Wreath

Oriental Heraldry

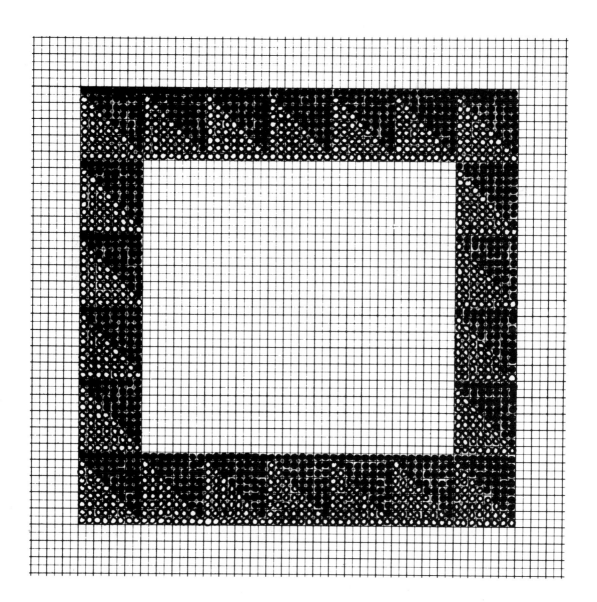

SECTION 6

Kitchens in Needlepoint

Asparagus Bouquet

Who ever thought that needlepoint would end up in the kitchen? Here are some carefree designs just for the kitchen—and *nobody* says they're just for company.

Materials: #12 interlock canvas, 8⅛″ by 6¼″
(design area, 5⅛″ by 3¼″)
½ yd. piping
recipe box* for 3″ by 5″ cards

Color Key and Thread Count

Key		Color	Skeins	Key		Color	Skeins
◨	895	Dark green	1	◘	947	Red orange	1
⊠	905	Medium green	2	⊡	606	Orange	1
⊡	907	Light green	1	**BG**	307	Yellow	2

Stitches: Continental, Basketweave

Finishing: Use Method A.

* See Appendix.

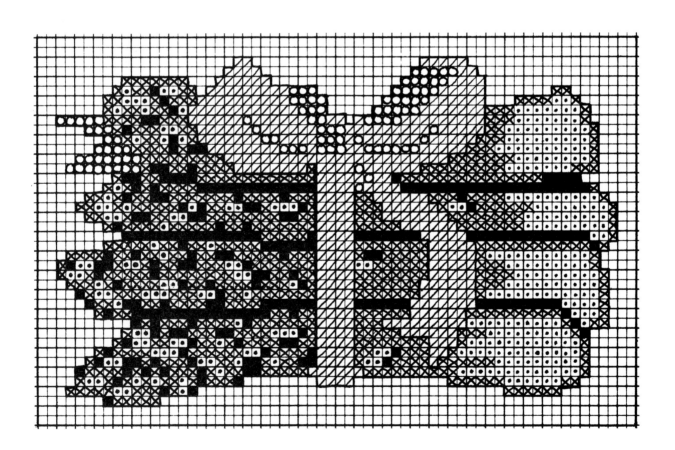

58

Artichoke Rose

Not only are artichokes delicious, but they are also as pretty as roses. This box can serve as a charming hideaway for lots of little goodies.

Materials: #12 interlock canvas, 7⅛″ by 7½″
(design area, 5⅛″ by 5½″)
wooden canister,* 5½″ by 6¾″
ceramic mushroom
⅔ yd. piping

Color Key and Thread Count

Key		Color	Skeins
■	895	Dark green	1
☒	904	Medium green	2
☐	905	Green	2
⊡	907	Light green	1
BG	307	Yellow	5

Stitches: Continental, Basketweave

Finishing: Use Method A.

* See Appendix.

59

The Big Carrot

The "Big Carrot" oven mitt definitely holds its own in this world of Big Apples and other popular designs. This practical project is a good introduction to the technique of needlepoint appliqué.

Materials: #12 interlock canvas, 11″ by 4⅝″
(design area, 9″ by 2⅝″)
quilted oven mitt

Color Key and Thread Count

Key	Color	Skeins
◘	947 Red orange	2
▨	606 Orange	1
■	895 Dark green	2
⊠	905 Medium green	2
⊡	907 Light green	2

Stitches: Continental, Basketweave

Finishing: This design has no background. Clip the corners all around. Fold canvas under, then stitch down, as shown in Method A. Appliqué the finished carrot right onto the oven mitt.

Hors D'Oeuvres on Parade (DAF)

This apron belongs in the winner's circle because it's both lovely and easy to care for. Don't overlook the possibility of using this band to create other culinary objets d'art. Use it as a band around your canisters or down the edge of a placemat, or even fixed to a spice or mug rack.

Materials: #12 interlock canvas, 33″ by 3½″
(design area, bib 9″ by 1½″, waist 20″ by 1½″)
yellow bib apron

Color Key and Thread Count

Key	Color	Skeins	Key	Color	Skeins
■	666 Red	3	▨	907 Light green	1
◘	606 Orange	2	⊟	434 Brown	1
⊡	947 Red orange	2	⊞	783 Gold	1
⊠	895 Dark green	1	□	712 Off-white	1
▨	905 Medium green	1	**BG**	307 Yellow	10

Stitches: Continental, Basketweave

Finishing: Use Method A.

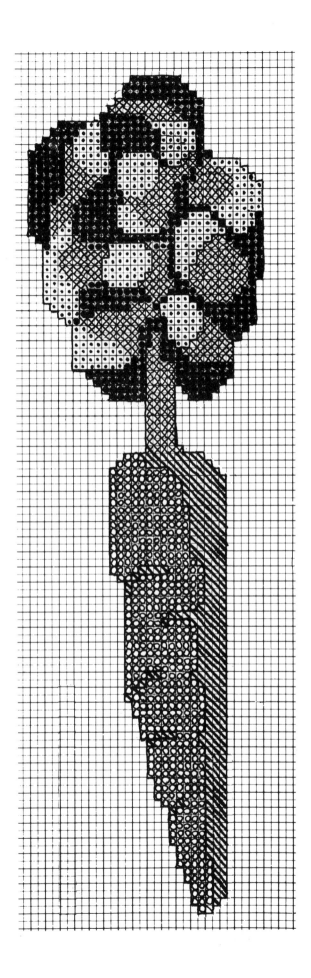

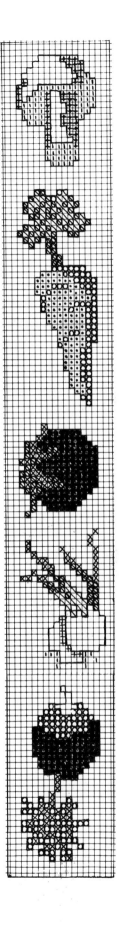

SECTION 7

Bathroom Highlights

Lily and the Frog (DAF)

This design belongs to what I call my bath menagerie. These creatures couldn't be easier to care for or more fun to decorate with.

Materials: #12 interlock canvas, 36″ by 4½″
(design area, 33¼″ by 2½″)
tissue box*

Color Key and Thread Count

Key	Color	Skeins	Key	Color	Skeins
⊡	776 Light pink	4	⊠	702 Medium green	4
◻	899 Medium pink	8	⊟	699 Dark green	8
◼	326 Dark pink	4	**BG**	310 Black	16
⊠	954 Light green	8			

Stitches: Continental, Basketweave, and French Knot (for frog's eye)

Finishing: Use Method A along with Zigzag stitch.

* See Appendix.

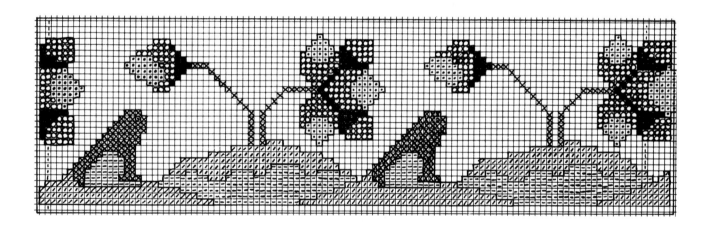

Jogging Turtles (DAF)

These "jogging" turtles on your bath mat may give a hint to the slowpokes in your family.

Materials: #6 canvas, 40″ wide by 44″ long; cut 4 strips 40″ long by 11″ wide; fold each strip in half—40″ long by 5½″ wide
(design area, 3½″ wide)
one bath mat approximately 22″ by 34″ (different brands are apt to vary slightly in size)
large darning needle
heavy rug yarn, 3.2 to 3.5 ounce skeins, labeled machine-washable and -dryable

Color Key and Thread Count

Key	Color	Skeins
■	Emerald green	1
⊡	Lime green	1
BG	White	2

Special Instructions: Pre-wash bath mat several times. Do not wash your #6 canvas prior to stitching, as it may soften and become difficult to work with. To chart the right layout for your size bath mat, consider one of the two layouts shown. Measure the number of inches in each strip and multiply that by 4 to find the number of stitches in each one. Every turtle is 19 stitches long and I used 5 spaces between mine, so each took 24 spaces. Divide your lengths by 24 to find the number of turtles per strip. You can adjust the number of spaces in order to make it fit your measurements. (Use the canvas doubled and save the folded edge to work in the Binding Stitch.) Most rug yarn can be used in single strands—test to be sure.

Stitches: Continental, Basketweave, Binding

Finishing: Fold the loose canvas edge under tightly so that none shows. Top stitch the border onto the edge of the bath mat by machine. Leave the overlapping border pieces loose and lay the mat down. Now baste the seams where the borders meet, being sure to leave the one row open all around for the Binding Stitch. Make any necessary adjustments, then machine stitch. Now work the Binding Stitch all around. Backing is optional.

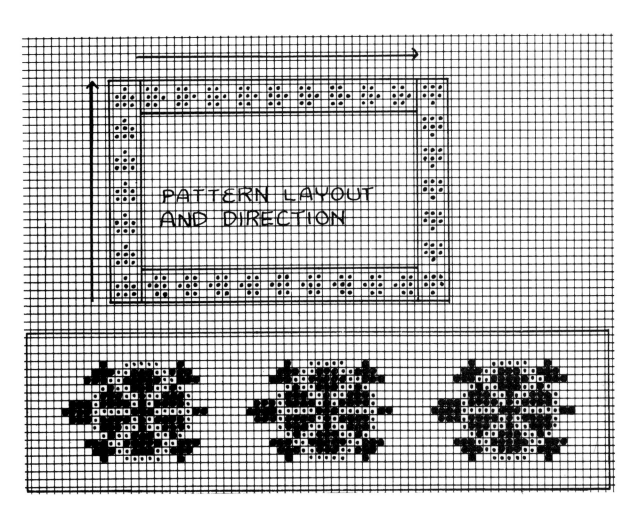

PATTERN LAYOUT
AND DIRECTION

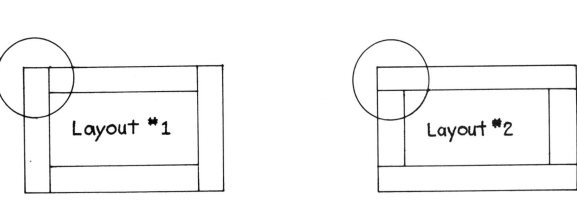

Layout #1

Layout #2

Butterflies Are Free

That may be true, but we can enjoy butterflies most when they alight close by. It's hard to believe that a design like this is so easy to care for!

Materials: #12 interlock canvas, 5⅝″ by 6⅛″
(design area, 3⅝″ by 4⅛″)
24″ piece gingham ribbon, 1½″ wide, gathered
waste can

Color Key and Thread Count

Key		Color	Skeins
☐	704	Light green	1
◼	699	Dark green	1
⊡		White	1
◲	601	Rose	1
BG	809	Blue	3

Stitches: Continental, Basketweave

Finishing: Use Method A.

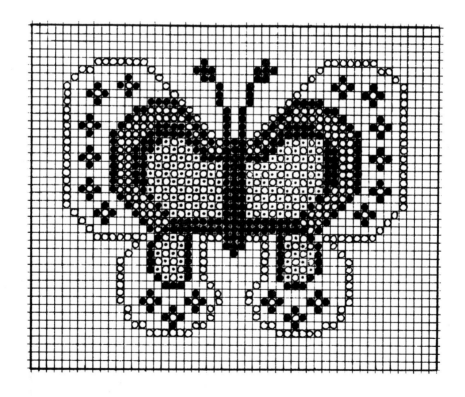

South on the Border (DAF)

One evening, a friend was looking over my projects; she was attracted to this design. As she picked it up she said jokingly, "How cute. Are these chickens on a dish towel?" What else can I say about this winsome design?

Materials: #12 interlock canvas, 13″ by 3⅝″
(design area, 11″ by 1⅝″)
⅔ yd. binding
guest towel (11″ wide)

Color Key and Thread Count

Key	Color	Skein
⊡	907 Light green	1
▨	905 Medium green	1
▩	895 Dark green	1
◎	307 Yellow	2
⊠	947 Orange	1
BG	White	4

Stitches: Continental, Basketweave

Finishing: Use Method A.

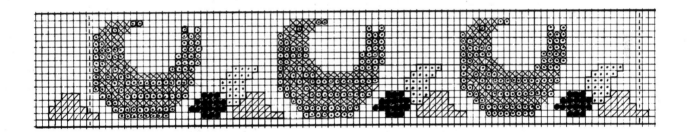

Monkey Business (DAF)

A perfect addition to the Bath Menagerie.

Materials: #12 interlock canvas, 7¼″ by 38″; cut into 2 strips, 3⅝″ by 38″ each
(design area, 1⅝″ by 72″)
shower curtain (plastic or fabric)

Color Key and Thread Count

Key	Color	Skeins
▢	434 Brown	7
◪	783 Tan	2
⊠	301 Rust	7
⊡	402 Light rust	2
◼	310 Black	11
BG	907 Green	28

Special Instructions: Splice

Stitches: Continental, Basketweave, and French Knot (monkeys' eyes)

Finishing: Use Method A. Stitch or glue onto shower curtain. A properly applied white glue is adequate, provided that the glued-on design is not subjected to constant soakings.

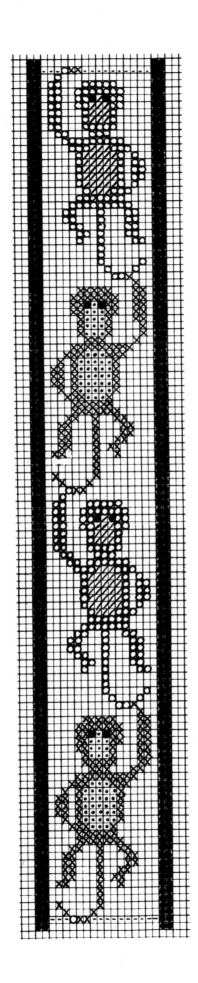

Snail's Pace

This snail's pace would be frustrating if he weren't so cute. He'll stay put through lots of washing and make every day special for you. After all, you deserve it!

Materials: #12 interlock canvas, 6″ by 5½″
(design area, 4″ by 3½″)
1 yd. yellow piping
1 yd. orange piping
1⅓ yd. red piping
one bath towel

Color Key and Thread Count

Key	Color	Skeins
●	919 Rust	1
⊠	606 Red	1
☐	947 Orange	1
⊡	741 Pale Orange	1
⊘	307 Yellow	1
⬓	3045 Tan	1
BG	907 Chartreuse	4

Stitches: Continental, Basketweave

Finishing: Use Method A.

SECTION 8

For Your Bedroom

Rosebud Ribbon (DAF)

This is such a darling way to tie back the curtains. It's as easy to care for as today's "old-fashioned" ruffled and lace curtains!

Materials: #12 interlock canvas, 3½" by 26" for 1 pair of tiebacks
(design area, 1⅝" by 11" for each tieback)
3 yd. grosgrain ribbon, 1⅝" wide

Color Key and Thread Count

Key	Color	Skeins	Key	Color	Skeins
☐	605 Light pink	1	⊠	701 Dark green	1
◼	602 Dark pink	1	⊡	809 Blue	2
⊞	704 Light green	1	**BG**	White	5

Stitches: Continental, Basketweave

Finishing: Use Method A. Cut your 3-yard length of ribbon in half. Fold the 1½ yards of grosgrain in half. Mark the center of the ribbon. Place one end of the needlepoint on that center and stitch down on all four sides. Cut the ends of the ribbon on the diagonal and dab a small amount of glue to the cut to prevent raveling.

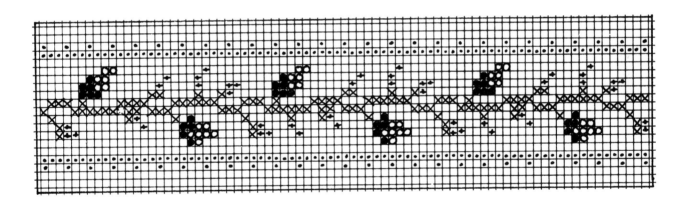

Sailor's Delight (DAF)

How sweet to close your eyes and dream of faraway places, with the gentle roll of the seas to rock you to sleep. Use the alphabet on page 126 to plot the name.

Materials: #12 interlock canvas, 7¼″ by 35″; cut lengthwise into 2 strips
(design area, 1⅝″ by 66″)
twin size washable blanket

Color Key and Thread Count

Key	Color	Skeins	Key	Color	Skeins
⊡	703 Green	2	◼	413 Gray	2
⊟	666 Red	2	⊠	947 Orange	2
⊡	307 Yellow	2	◻	797 Sea blue	8
☐	White	8	**BG**	800 Sky blue	28

Special Instructions: Splice and Monogram

Stitches: Continental, Basketweave

Finishing: Use Method A.

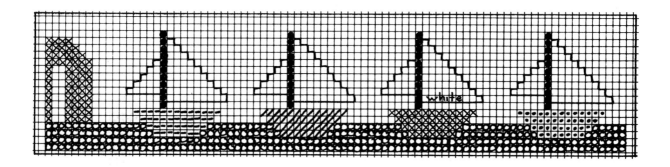

Hearts and Flowers (DAF)

This border is so dressy that it's hard to believe it's for everyday use. It is easy to personalize by using the 8 × 8 alphabet on page 127. Center your name on the border and then add as many hearts and flowers as you need.

Materials: #12 interlock canvas, 3½" by 23"
(design area, 1½" by 21")
1½ yd. polyester eyelet lace
one standard pillowcase

Color Key and Thread Count

Key	Color	Skeins
■	799 Blue	1
·	307 Yellow	2
▢	891 Red	2
⊠	703 Green	2
BG	White	5

Special Instructions: Monogram

Stitches: Continental, Basketweave

Finishing: Use Method A, including eyelet lace.

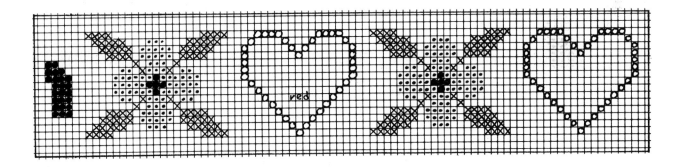

Rosebud Monogram

What a charming and delicate way to dress up a wastebasket! The most attractive feature is its practicality.

Materials: #12 interlock canvas, 5½″ by 5½″
(design area, 3½″ by 3½″)
wastebasket
½ yd. polyester eyelet lace
⅔ yd. dark green ⅝″ grosgrain ribbon
enough 1⅝″ grosgrain ribbon to border top and bottom of wastebasket

Color Key and Thread Count

Key	Color	Skeins
■	602 Dark pink	1
◘	604 Light pink	1
⊠	699 Dark green	1
⊞	703 Light green	1
BG	White	3

Special Instructions: Monogram

Stitches: Continental, Basketweave

Finishing: Use Method A.

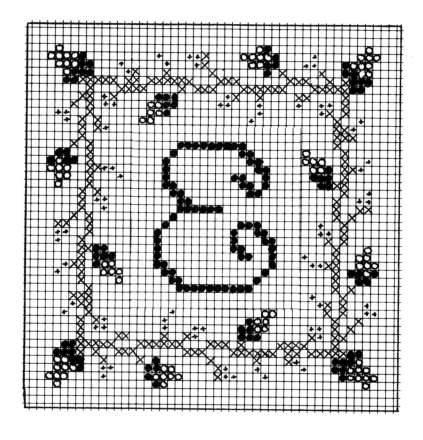

Butterfly Looking Glass

The butterfly's colors ripple so softly against the strong greens, it seems as if its wings are almost fluttering.

Materials: #12 interlock canvas, 6½″ by 6½″
(design area, 4⅜″ in diameter)
a hand mirror that can accommodate a 4½″-diameter design area

Color Key and Thread Count

Key	Color	Skeins
◘	909 Dark green	2
■	517 Dark blue	1
☐	992 Medium blue	1
⊡	827 Light blue	1
BG	703 Light green	3

Stitches: Continental, Basketweave

Finishing: Use Method A.

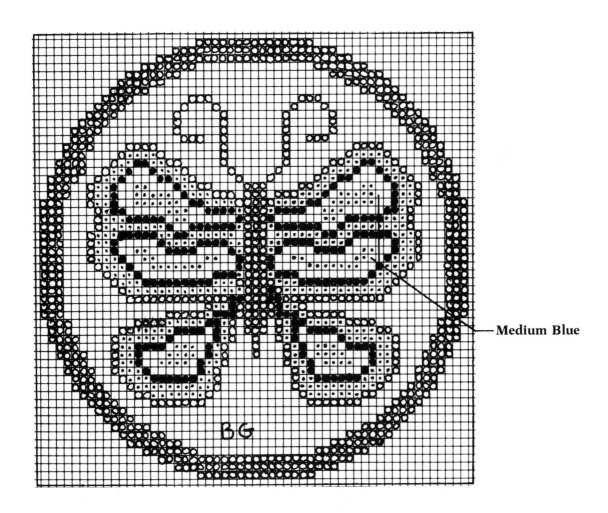

— Medium Blue

SECTION 9

Just For Fun:
Games, Accessories
and Other Diversions

Pups' and Kitties' Flea Collars

I won't promise that these collars can repel a single insect, but I do know your pet will be the best dressed, with a snappy army of fleas marching around on its personalized collar!

LARGE COLLAR
Materials: #12 interlock canvas, pet's neck size plus 6″ by 3″
(design area, neck size plus 5″ by 1″)
1″ buckle and keeper
1″ belt backing the length of the collar

Color Key and Thread Count (Medium fits up to 14″; Large fits up to 20″)

Key	Color	Skeins		Key	Color	Skeins	
		M	L			M	L
◼	947 Orange	3	4	⊠	801 Brown*	1	1
⊡	725 Gold	2	3	**BG**	436 Tan	5	6

SMALL COLLAR
Materials: #18 interlock canvas, pet's neck size plus 5″ by 3″
(design area, neck size plus 3½″ by ½″)
½″ buckle and keeper
½″ seam binding the length of the collar

Color Key and Thread Count (Small fits up to 10″; Medium fits up to 14″)

Key	Color	Skeins		Key	Color	Skeins	
		S	M			S	M
⊡	353 Peach	1	1		351 Brick*	2	3
◼	817 Dark peach	1	1	**BG**	519 Blue	2	3

Special Instructions: Use a piece of string to measure your pet's neck. The string should be loose enough to allow two of your fingers to fit under it easily. This measurement determines the length from the center of the buckle to the middle eyelet. The narrow and the wide collars are illustrated in Fig. 19.

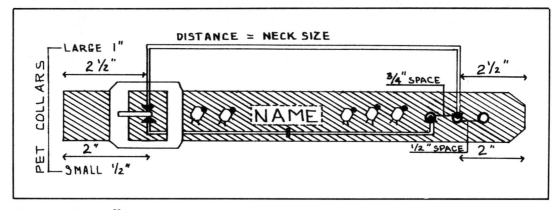

Fig. 19. Pet Collars

* Also used for fleas' legs and eyes.

(1.) Mark off both ends as illustrated. (2.) Find the center between the end marks and plot your pet's name using the alphabet on page 127. (3.) Mark eyelets as shown. (4.) Add fleas, spacing them evenly between the buckle and the first eyelet. (5.) Make a pattern for the buttonhole from stiff paper to insure that the prong can move freely. See drawing for suggestions on size.

Stitches: Use embroidery floss as usual for #12 canvas. Use only single floss for #18 canvas. Use Continental, Basketweave, Buttonhole/Eyelet, French Knot (eyes), and Overlay (legs).

Finishing: Block. Cut open buttonhole and eyelets carefully! Use Method A. Topstitch the buckle end twice. Slip the buckle onto the finished collar and stitch down twice. Thread the keeper over the open end and secure by stitching down twice. (See Fig. 20.)

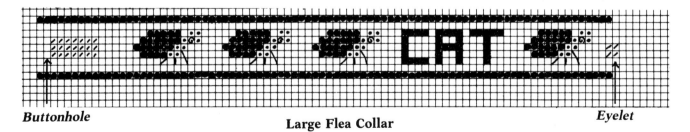

Fig. 20. Machine Stitching

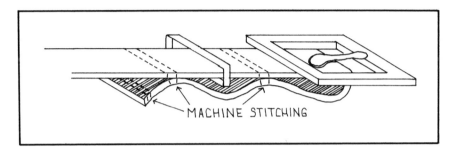

Small Flea Collar

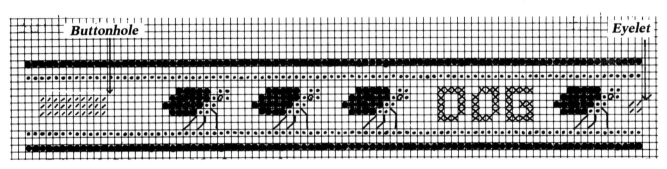

Buttonhole   **Large Flea Collar**   *Eyelet*

HOLIDAYS

Birds and Berries Holiday Wreath

I have drawn from the bounty of nature for this rich holiday design. The nature of needlepoint itself allows this traditional welcome sign to become a treasured heirloom.

Materials: #12 interlock canvas, 16″ by 16″
(design area, 12″ in diameter)
½ yd. red fabric for backing and piping
⅝ yd. grosgrain ribbon, 1⅝″ wide
polyester fiber-fill

Color Key and Thread Count

Key	Color		Skeins
◘	703	Light green	8
⊠	699	Dark green	6
◙	498	Red	1
■	310	Black	4
⊡	415	Light gray	2
◪	414	Dark gray	2
BG	712	Ecru	20

Stitches: Continental, Basketweave, and French Knot (red)

Finishing: Use Method B. Add a loop of piping to use as a hanger.

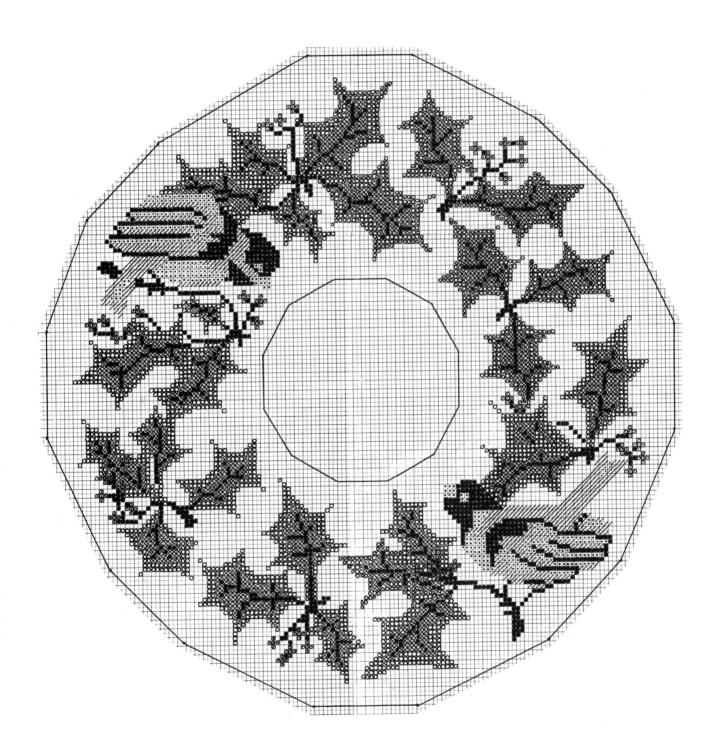

Christmas Tree Ornaments

The sentiments of holiday seasons are well remembered in my own collection of tree ornaments. Every one is a treasure to me, especially those from friends in Christmases past. The next 6 designs were chosen from a collection of 24 patterns.* Why not begin now, adding your initials and the date to these ornaments—it's such a lovely way to begin a tradition.

Materials: #12 interlock canvas, 4″ by 4″ each
felt squares for backing

SANTA
Color Key and Thread Count

Key	Color		Skeins
◘	666	Red	1
■	797	Blue	1
◪	754	Flesh	1
◉		White	1
BG	701	Green	1

Special Instructions: Use French Knots for white in Santa's beard and trim on his hat.

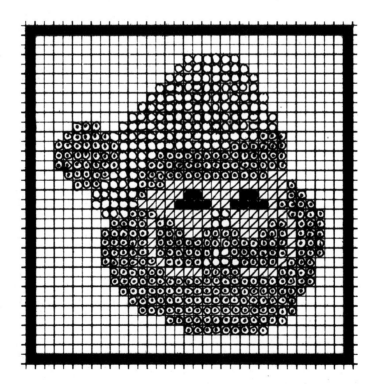

* See Appendix.

ANGEL
Color Key and Thread Count

Key	Color		Skeins
⊡	799	Light blue	1
■	797	Dark blue	1
▢	307	Deep yellow	1
⊗		Metallic gold**	1
⧄	754	Flesh	1
⊠	434	Brown	1
BG		White	1

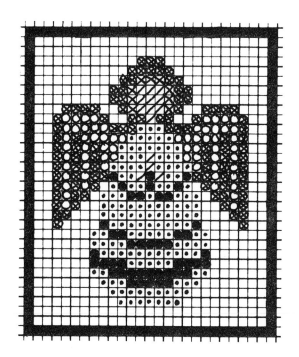

THE LION
Color Key and Thread Count

Key	Color		Skeins
⊡	783	Gold	1
◉	919	Russet	1
BG	701	Green	1
◎		Tweed	

Special Instructions: Make Tweed yarn with one strand gold and one strand russet for French Knot for lion's mane.

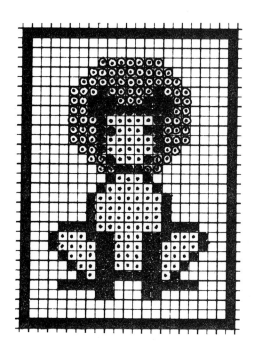

THE LAMB
Color Key and Thread Count

Key		Color	Skeins
⊡	415	Light gray	1
⊠	414	Dark gray	1
■	310	Black	1
BG	907	Light green	1
◉		Tweed	

Special Instructions: Make Tweed yarn with one strand light gray and one strand dark gray for French Knot for lamb's wool.

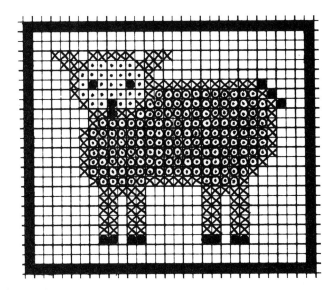

CHRISTMAS TREE
Color Key and Thread Count

Key		Color	Skeins
◻	666	Red	1
⊠	797	Blue	1
⊡	701	Green	1
⊗		Metallic gold**	1
BG		White	1

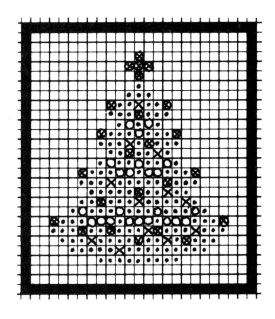

** Make test stitches with metallic thread to determine the right number of strands for this canvas.

GOD'S EYE
Color Key and Thread Count

Key	Color		Skeins
⊡	666	Red	1
⊟	947	Orange	1
◻	307	Yellow	1
⬛	797	Blue	1
⊠	552	Purple	1
BG and ◹	701	Green	1

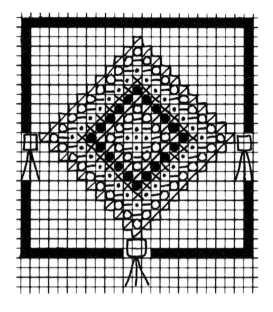

Stitches: Continental, Basketweave, French Knot, and Binding

Finishing: Double a 12-inch metallic or floss hanger thread and stitch through the top center before finishing using Method A and Binding. To make tassels for God's Eye: For each tassel, wrap floss five times around two fingers, then slip tie through the loops. Tie loops together as shown and clip at bottom. (See Fig. 21.)

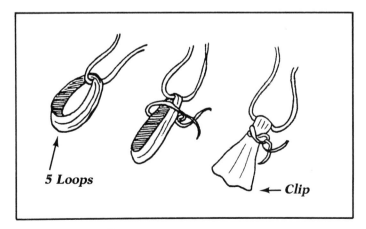

Fig. 21.   Tassels

GAMES

Backgammon Graphics

Note that this pattern shows only one side of a backgammon board. It must be stitched twice for a complete board.

One of the most popular games today is backgammon. I have utilized the symmetry of its board, together with the letters of its name, to create this handsome graphic design. This game is custom bound with oiled walnut, but the dimensions given here coincide with the size of the frame listed in the Appendix.

Materials: #12 interlock canvas, 26″ by 17½″
(design area, 2 pieces, 9″ by 13½″ each)
optional frame*, 16″ by 24″
optional playing set: men, dice, doubler, and cups*

Color Key and Thread Count

	Key		Color	Skeins
Red	{	□	946 Terra cotta	12
points	{	◻	919 Brick**	18
Green	{	□	469 Moss	12
points	{	⊠	895 Forest	18
	BG		783 Bronze	21

Special Instructions: Work each half separately for your convenience.

Stitches: Continental, Basketweave

Finishing: Have the board custom framed; or, if you decide to purchase one, be certain of its dimensions before completing the stitching.

  * See Appendix.
** Also used for the border.

The World's Greatest

Here is a definite winner! You will enjoy this game even if your spelling is as awful as mine! If you want to create your own cryptic message, the alphabet used appears on page 127.

Materials: #12 interlock canvas, 15″ by 15″
(design area, 11″ by 11″)
plastic Parsons table 16″ by 16″
mat board 15″ by 15″
⅛″ clear plastic, 16″ by 16″, for top
felt circles (the kind used under glass table-top covers)

Color Key and Thread Count

Key		Color	Skeins	Key	Color	Skeins
L	N	809 Light blue	4	R	602 Red	2
B	I	798 Dark blue	2	■	310 Black	16
P	Z	605 Light pink	3	BG	White*	25

Stitches: Continental, Basketweave

Finishing: Use Method A. Trim canvas to have a 1-inch border. Tape canvas to table. Cut the mat to fit snugly to the edge of the canvas. Hold the mat down with double-edged tape. You will then have a ½-inch white border all around. Stack the felt circles 2 or 3 together and secure them with rubber cement to keep the plastic top in place.

* Use also for letters on dark blue and red squares.

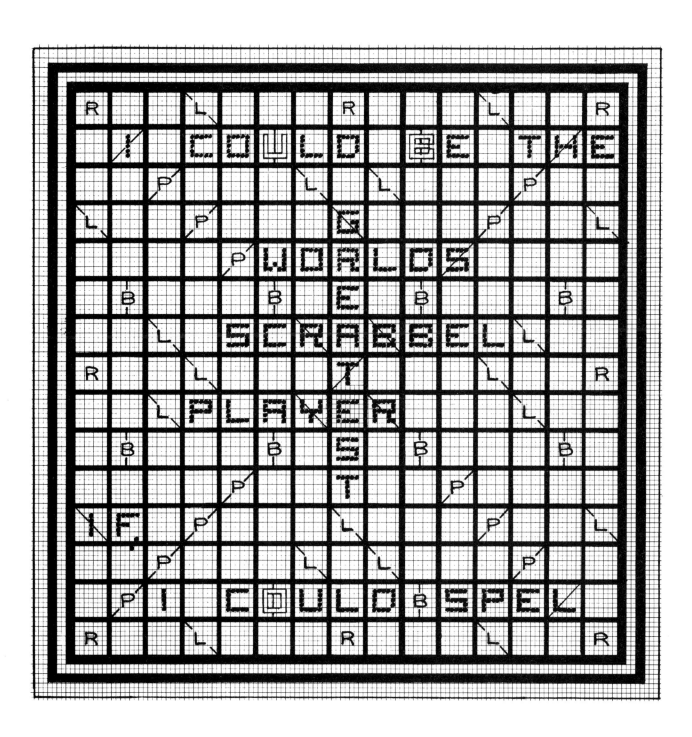

Grass Roots

We all know that tennis shoes are no longer confined to the courts, but liberation is not enough. Our goal was to create the most desirable—that is washable—decoration for tennis shoes; that's what Grass Roots is all about!

Materials: #12 interlock canvas, 18″ by 40″
(design area, see pattern)

Color Key and Thread Count

Key	Color	Skeins
■	699 Dark green	36
⊡	666 Red	1
⊠	310 Black	1
BG	704 Light green	42

Stitches: Continental, Basketweave

Special Instructions: One size fits all. Make two of each pattern. The wide bottom border allows for adjustment to your size. Be sure to mark each piece of the canvas so the stitch direction is consistent over the whole design.

Finishing: See Appendix.

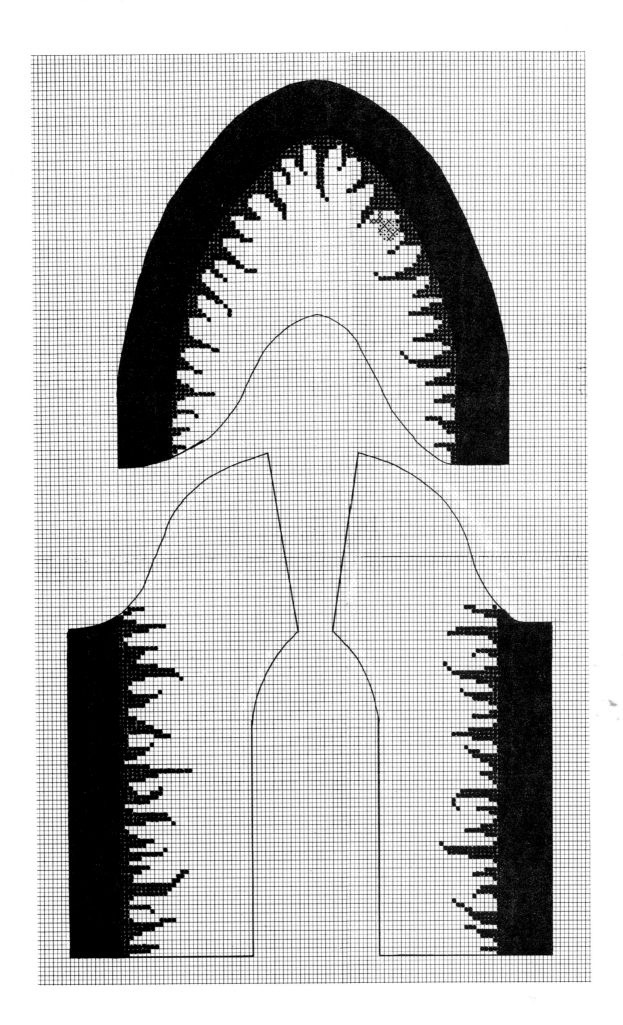

Sunshine

This is one of the greatest of all "smiling faces." You can't help but improve your tennis game (and your smile) having him on your side.

Materials: pre-finished tennis racquet cover with #12 interlock canvas*

Color Key and Thread Count

Key	Color	Skeins	Key	Color	Skeins
A and *a*	726 Yellow	9	*1*	954 Pale green	5
B	742 Peach	4	*2*	907 Light green	9
C and ⊠	740 Orange	5	*3*	702 Kelly	10
D and ◼	947 Red orange	9	*4*	905 Hunter	10
			5	909 Dark green	5

Stitches: Continental, Basketweave, Gobelin 3 (A, B, C, D), Gobelin/Diagonal (green background)

Finishing: Block and finish according to the directions for the pre-finished racquet cover.

* See Appendix.

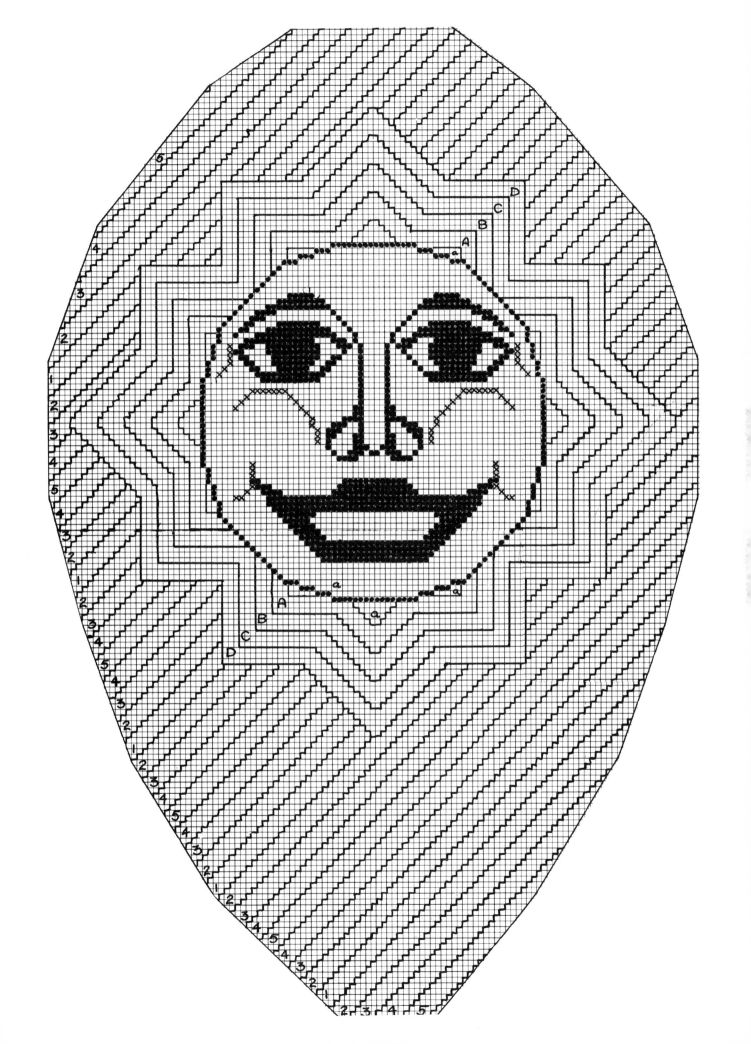

What's Your Game

Just pick your favorite design, add a monogram (see p. 127) if desired, and you will automatically be in the winner's circle, no matter what your game. Your comfort is provided for as well, with the open background canvas. Now that's "match point"!

Materials: #12 interlock canvas, 6½″ by 9″
ready-made tennis hat

IT'S THE BERRIES
Color Key and Thread Count

Key		Color	Skeins
◻	666	Red	1
▧	603	Pink	1
⊡	703	Medium green	1
▦	701	Dark green	1

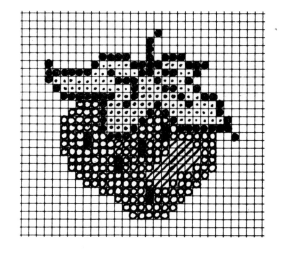

FLOWER
Color Key and Thread Count

Key		Color	Skeins
⊡	307	Yellow	1
◻	947	Orange	1
▦	701	Green	1

OVER THE BOUNDING MAIN
Color Key and Thread Count

Key	Color	Skeins
◨	666 Red	1
■	797 Blue	1
⊡	White	1

IT'S A BIRDIE
Color Key and Thread Count

Key	Color	Skeins
☑	666 Red	1
⊠	310 Black	1
⊡	White	1
◨	701 Light green	1
■	909 Dark green	1

 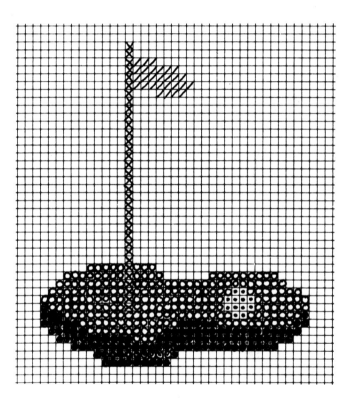

Stitches: Continental, Basketweave, Monogram

Special Instructions and Finishing: Carefully remove the two side panels of the hat, leaving the bias tape attached to the hat. Use these panels as patterns, allowing an extra ½ inch all around. Test your canvas to be sure it will not become completely limp after wetting and drying. Mark your design choice and monogram on the canvas. Stitch, being careful not to carry threads across the back, for the background is to be left open for ventilation. Now trim the worked canvas just slightly larger than the pattern. Fold forward the bias tape from the adjoining panels, and baste. Slip the canvas between the next panel and the folded bias tape. Trim the canvas if necessary. Baste first, then sew together by hand, choosing decorative or blind stitches in a matching or contrasting color.

PURSES

Bugs and Such (DAF)

This pattern is very versatile—it can be used horizontally or vertically. The multicolor scheme is perfect on this charming wooden purse.

Materials: #12 interlock canvas, 30″ by 3½″
(design area, 24″ by 1½″)
needlepointed ladybug, 1¼″ by 1½″
oval wooden purse*

Color Key and Thread Count

Key	Color	Skeins	Key	Color	Skeins
⊠	703 Medium green	1	◻	318 Gray	1
⊡	326 Dark rose	1	⧄	699 Dark green	1
⊘	352 Light rose	1	⊟	White	1
☐	598 Aqua	1	◼	310 Black	2
⊞	307 Yellow	1	**BG**	738 Fawn	8

Stitches: Continental, Basketweave, Overlay stitch, and 310 Black for French Knot

Finishing: Use Method A. Glue finished band to purse and tack ends of border together with Zigzag stitch.

* See Appendix.

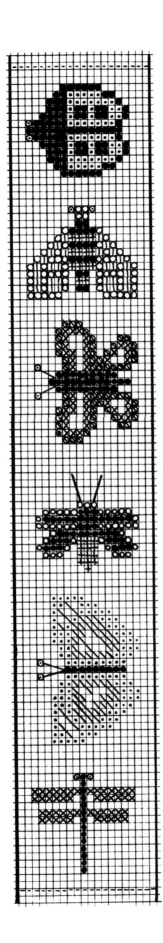

Rocky

Who can resist the charm of these "masked bandits"? The application of washable and dryable needlepoint is perfect for the "Bermuda bag" purse because the cover is removable. It is also far more economical than buying a custom-made bag. My buttonhole technique was designed originally for this project.

Materials: #12 interlock canvas, 26" by 16½"
front and back, each 13" by 11"; gusset, 5½" by 23"
(design area, front and back, each 10" by 8"; gusset, 2½" by 20")
Bermuda bag handle, 4-button*
½ yd. light cotton blend for facing
2 yd. piping

Color key and Thread Count

Key		Color	Skeins	Key	Color	Skeins
FRONT DESIGN						
⊠ and Ⓐ		801 Dark brown	2	▨	762 Pearl gray	1
Ⓑ		780 Medium brown	2	⊡	415 Light gray	2
Ⓒ		3045 Light brown	2	⊡	414 Medium gray	2
◼		310 Black	1	◻	413 Charcoal	1
◉		White	1	**BG**	906 Green	21
GUSSET		906 Green	20			
BACK		906 Green	29			

Special Instructions: Mark and stitch buttonholes first. Feel confident to adjust spacing for buttonholes according to your purse. Note that Light gray and Medium gray are to be worked together in the Tweed manner (see Glossary). Use the French Knot stitch for the eyes.

Stitches: Continental, Basketweave, Buttonhole, French Knot, and Gobelin 2, 3, 4, 5

Finishing: Use Method B. Make four buttonholes in each facing to correspond to those in both sides; then tack facing on top edges. Stitch facing to sides and bottom on front and back, leaving tops tacked for now. Stitch facing to gusset. Stitch piping around all sides of front and back. Turn inside out and stitch gusset to both sides. Turn right side out, test the fit of the cover on the handles, and make any necessary adjustments. Turn facing (and gusset also if need be) under, and sew a finished edge. Do this also on the tops of the front and back. You may want to substitute a plain fabric for the back and gusset.

* See Appendix.

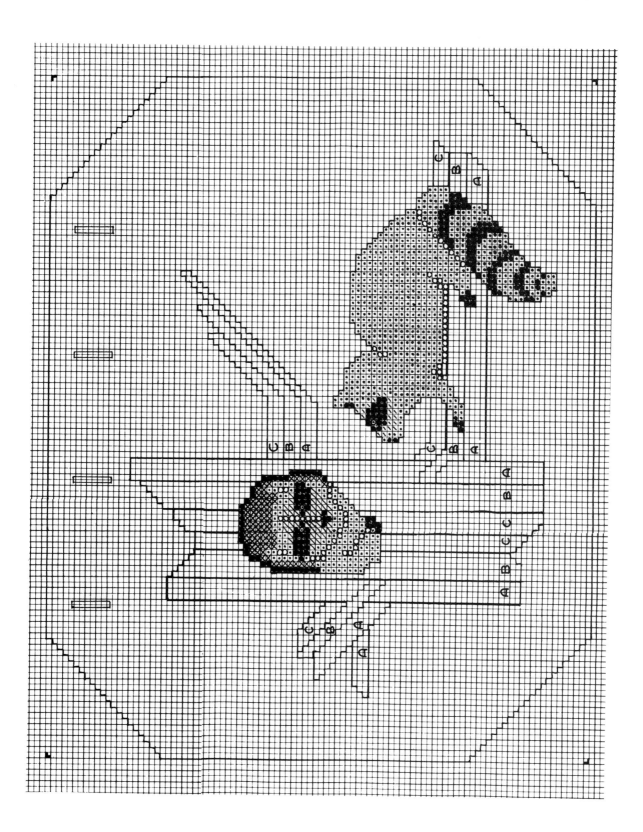

ACCESSORIES

Afrique

This particular design seems to attract attention no matter where it goes, and it can go anywhere! It is perfect as a pillow, or framed on the wall, or as a tote. The short-handled tote shown in the illustration is being used as a needlepoint carrier. A shoulder-length strap makes it great for carrying books and other things with ease and lots of pride.

Materials: #12 interlock canvas, 18″ by 18″
(design area, 14″ by 14″)
1 yd. heavy fabric (duck or canvas)
1⅔ yd. grosgrain ribbon 1⅝″ wide

Color Key and Thread Count

Key	Color	Skeins	Key	Color	Skeins
⊠	919 Rust	2	*F*	712 Ivory	1
G	922 Light rust	1	*D*	744 Cream	1
⊡	783 Gold	2	*A* and ▨	781 Light brown	3
E	415 Light gray	4	*B*	907 Light green	12
▨	414 Dark gray	2	*C*	701 Medium green	12
▢	434 Brown	4	■	310 Black	1
			BG	699 Dark green	50

Stitches: Continental, Basketweave, and French Knot (for animals' eyes)

Finishing: Use Method A. (See Fig. 22.) (A) Stitch finished canvas to tote front. (B) Decide handle length; stitch gusset and handle pieces together. (C) Sew gusset to front and back. (D) Turn under top edges and face with 1⅝-inch grosgrain. Face the underside of the handle with grosgrain.

Finished Measurements Tote: 14″ by 14″
Gusset/handle: 1¾″ by 66″ long (for shoulder bag)
Gusset/handle: 1¾″ by 60″ short (handbag)

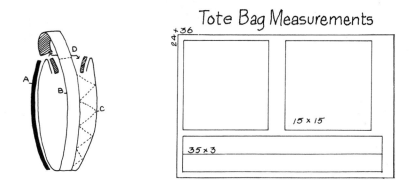

Fig. 22.   Finishing Details

On the Green (DAF)

This is an easy and inexpensive way to make a belt—and don't forget about all the other "Designs-A-Foot" patterns throughout the book from which you can choose. The information given below is based on a 28-inch design area. Why not add a monogram for good luck?

Materials: #12 interlock canvas, design area plus 4" by 3⅝"
(design area equals length by 1⅝")
clasp*, sized for 1½" width
backing for finishing (grosgrain or bias tape)

Color Key and Thread Count

Key	Color	Skeins	Key	Color	Skeins
◨	307 Yellow	1	⊡	703 Light green	3
⊠	666 Red	1	▢	701 Dark green	3
⊟	797 Blue	1	**BG**	519 Light blue	13**
◕	310 Black	1			

Special Instructions: See Belts in the glossary for how to measure and select materials.

Stitches: Continental, Basketweave

Finishing: Use Method A, Belts.

* See Appendix.
**Add 1 skein for every 2 inches in length.

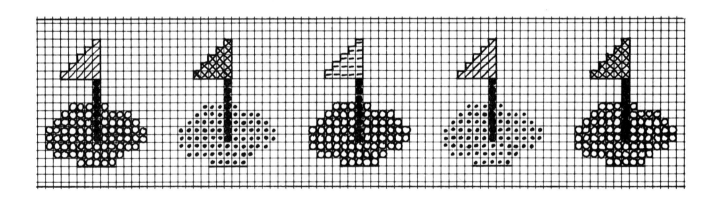

Rainbow Geometrics (DAF)

This design can be the finishing touch as a belt, overall straps, or suspenders. (Be sure to decide on the item before you begin.) The information given below is based on a 27-inch design area.

Materials: #12 interlock canvas, design area plus 4″ by 3¼″
(design area equals length by 1¼″)
hardware* for 1¼″ width
backing for finishing (grosgrain, bias tape)

Color Key and Thread Count

Key	Color	Skeins	Key	Color	Skeins
⊡	891 Red	2	■	799 Blue	2
⊟	740 Orange	2	⊠	553 Purple	2
◻	726 Yellow	2	**BG**	3045 Tan	9**
⧄	703 Green	2			

Special Instructions: See Belts in the glossary to measure for belts, suspenders, or overall straps, and for selection of materials.

Stitches: Continental, Basketweave

Finishing: Use Method A, Belts.

  * See Appendix.
  ** Add 1 skein for every 3 inches in length.

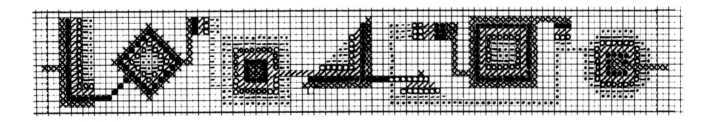

El Placebo

This dummy cigarette is better than the real thing. It will amuse your friends and is better for you than biting your fingernails or eating all the hors d'oeuvres yourself.

Materials: #12 interlock canvas, 3″ by 5″
(design area, 1⅛″ by 4″)
5″ length of clothesline
1 red felt-tip pen

Color Key and Thread Count

Key	Color	Skeins
☐	White	1
☒	738 Gold	1
◼	413 Charcoal	1

Stitches: Continental, Basketweave

Finishing: Trim canvas to ¼ inch on all sides. Fold ends down first; fold sides next. Lay rope down and roll the canvas around, matching the rows. Close the seam with doubled sewing thread, using a Zigzag stitch. Allowing ¼-inch rope out at "flame," color rope briskly with red pen. Making sure all the frayed rope is colored, pull it back into the "cigarette," leaving ⅛ inch protruding. Cut off other end of rope as close as possible. A gentle tug on the flame will give the filter a nice tight end.

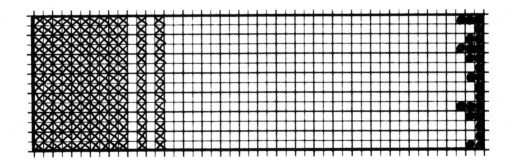

Egyptian Eye

For centuries, this symbolic design has been respected. I have combined its graphics with handsome colors and basic practicality to give you a key ring which is definitely a cut above the others. The back side is monogrammed using the alphabet on page 126 — it fits perfectly!

Materials: #12 interlock canvas, 11¼″ by 4¼″
(design area, 9¼″ by 2¼″)
self-lock key ring, 1½″ in diameter

Color Key and Thread Count

Key	Color	Skeins
⊡	307 Yellow	1
◼	820 Navy	2
BG	701 Kelly green	5

Special Instructions: Monogram

Stitches: Continental, Basketweave

Finishing: Use Method A. Work Binding stitch on narrow center first. Next, roll canvas lengthwise and slip key ring on. Fold canvas in half and work both sides together with the Binding stitch. Anchor the last thread by working it back and forth in between the canvases.

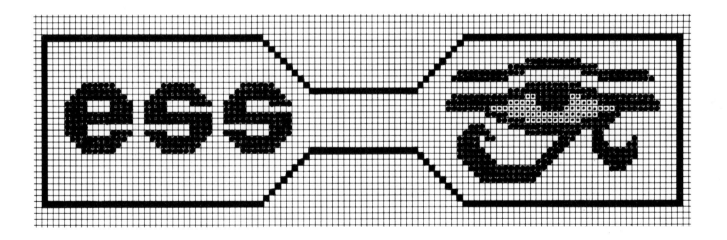

The Mouse Takes the Cheese

If you have trouble finding your keys, then this little fellow can be just the right answer. There is room for your monogram on the other side.

Materials: #12 interlock canvas
key ring, 9½″ by 3¼″
(design area, 7½″ by 1¼″)
key holder, 4½″ by 4½″
(design area, 2½″ by 2½″)
small wooden plaque* with 2¾″ face diameter
self-lock key ring, 1″ in diameter
small brass cup hook
¾ yd. piping

Color Key and Thread Count

Key	Color	Skeins	Key	Color	Skeins
⊡	973 Yellow	1	⊿	414 Gray	1
◻	972 Light orange	1	⊠	310 Black	1
⬤	971 Orange	1	**BG**	747 Blue	3

Special Instructions: Monogram

Stitches: Continental, Basketweave

Finishing: Use Method A. Roll canvas to accommodate the metal ring. Fold canvas in half and stitch the "necks" of the key ring together. Place the piping in between the sides and stitch through all three layers. I used a decorative orange saddle stitch over my machine-stitching.

* See Appendix.

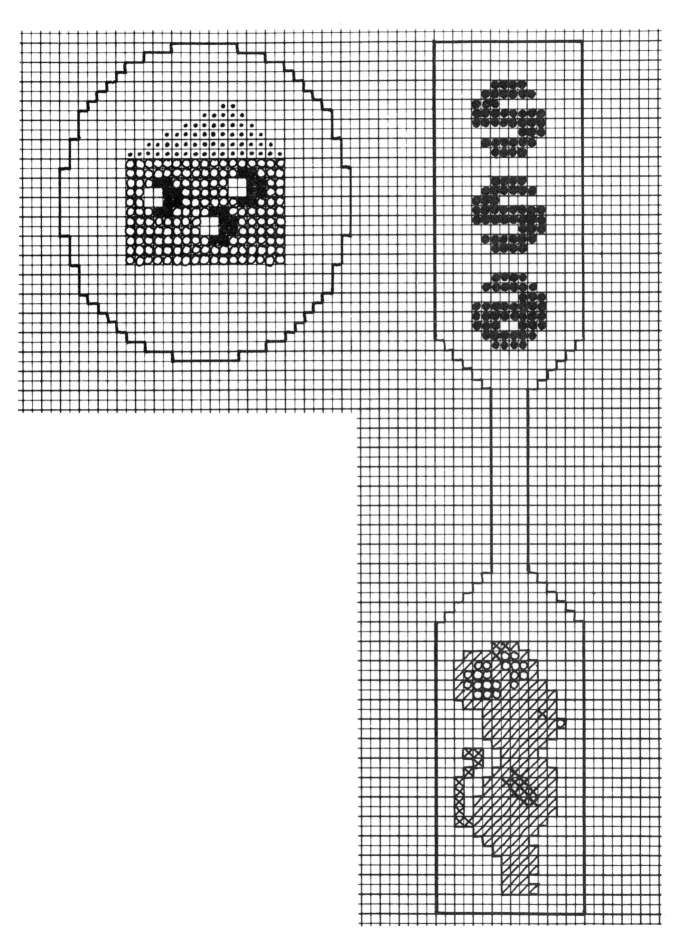

Gumballs Galore

This is a great box to stash your pennies in. Time was, you could buy one or even two gumballs for a penny. Oh well, while you save up, stitch this quick and easy project because it's worth it.

Materials: #12 interlock canvas 5″ by 6″
(design area, 3″ by 4″)
painted or stained box* (minimum size 3½″ by 4½″)
one red ceramic drawer knob
⅔ yd. binding

Color Key and Thread Count

Key	Color	Skeins	Key	Color	Skeins
⊠	797 Blue	1	▱	307 Yellow	1
▢	666 Red	1	⊡	701 Green	1
■	413 Gray	1	**BG**	White	3

Stitches: Continental, Basketweave

Finishing: Use Method A.

* See Appendix.

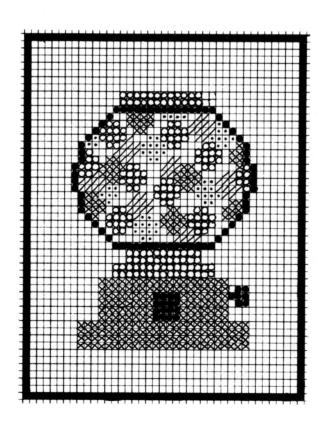

Pot o' Gold

Here is a very contemporary cachepot that you may never fill with gold, but at least you will enjoy having it or making it for a gift.

Materials: #12 interlock canvas, 5″ by 6″
(design area, 3″ by 4″)
½ yd. piping
painted or stained wooden box,* 4½″ by 5⅝″

Color Key and Thread Count

Key	Color	Skeins	Key	Color	Skeins
⊡	666 Red	1	◼	797 Blue	1
⊟	947 Orange	1	⊠	552 Purple	1
◖	307 Yellow	1	**BG**	800 Light blue	3
☐	701 Green	1			

Stitches: Continental, Basketweave

Finishing: Use Method A.

* See Appendix.

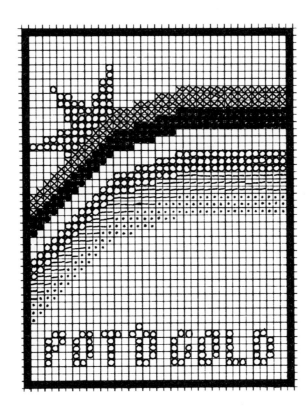

Walking Tall

That's exactly what this little fellow is doing. He's just the right size for my glasses—what a happy coincidence!

Materials: #12 interlock canvas, 8″ by 8½″
(design area, 6″ by 6½″)
10″ by 10″ piece soft fabric for lining

Color Key and Thread Count

Key	Color	Skeins	Key	Color	Skeins
⊠	907 Light green	2	⊡	745 Cream	1
◼	909 Dark green	2	⊘	783 Gold	3
◻	919 Russet	4	**BG**	519 Sky blue	6

Special Instructions: Monogram

Stitches: Continental, Basketweave, Binding

Finishing: Trim canvas to ½ inch and fold under, leaving one folded row exposed to accommodate the Binding stitch. Lay the lining fabric over the back of the canvas. Turn under as you tack it along the edges, leaving the one row of canvas free. Do the Binding stitch on the top border of the canvas. Fold the whole piece in half and bind the side and bottom edges together as you stitch.

Oriental Heraldry

This set of handsome coasters was inspired by authentic oriental family crests. They also make beautiful pictures when framed.

Materials: #12 interlock canvas, 6″ by 6″ for each coaster, or 6″ by 36″
(design area, 4″ by 4″ each)
felt backing 4″ by 4″ each, or 1 sq. ft.

Color Key and Thread Count *(for Entire Set)*

Key		Color	Skeins
⊡	399	Light red	3
◨	326	Medium red	6
◼	3685	Dark red	3
⧄	954	Light green	3
⊟	911	Medium green	4
⊠	909	Dark green	2
BG	712	Ecru	26

Stitches: Continental, Basketweave, Binding

Finishing: Use Method A. Apply coasters to felt backing with rubber cement.

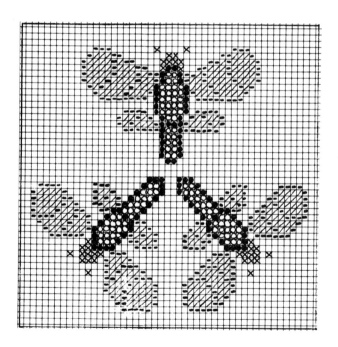
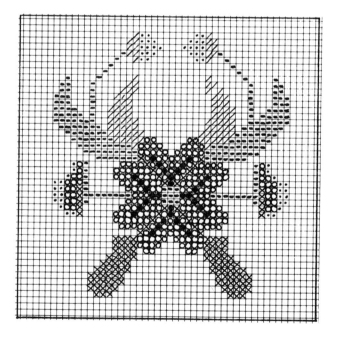

116

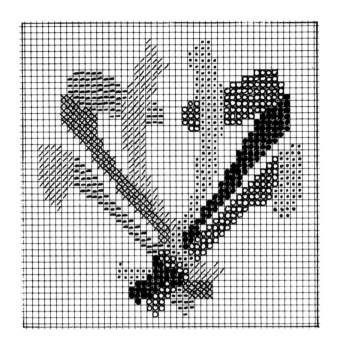

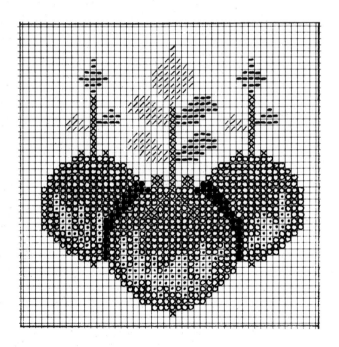

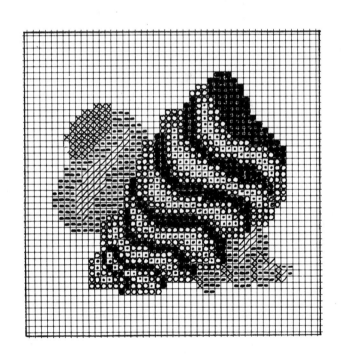

Budding Vine (DAF)

This dainty little border provides a dash of color for those lovely foliage plants. The small box will fit perfectly on your window sill.

Materials: #12 interlock canvas, 8″ by 3″
(design area, 6″ by ⅞″)
flower box,* 3½″ by 4¾″

Color Key and Thread Count

Key	Color	Skeins
◘	947 Red orange	1
⊡	972 Light orange	1
⊠	907 Light green	1
◕	701 Dark green	1
BG	747 Aqua	1

Stitches: Continental, Basketweave

Finishing: Use Method A.

*See Appendix.

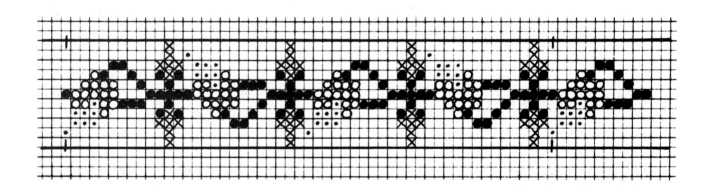

Garden Border (DAF)

This pattern is soft and delicate. It would look just as nice decorating your belt, a finger towel, a curtain, or a flower box.

Materials: #12 interlock canvas, 3¾" by 28"
(design area, 1¾" by 26")
wooden box* (ours is 6½" by 7¾")
1½ yd. lime grosgrain ribbon, ⅝" wide

Color Key and Thread Count

Key	Color	Skeins	Key	Color	Skeins
⊞	894 Pink	1	⊠	703 Light green	2
⊡	893 Light red	1	■	701 Dark green	1
◘	891 Dark red	1	**BG**	738 Tan	6

Stitches: Continental, Basketweave

Finishing: Use Method A.

* See Appendix.

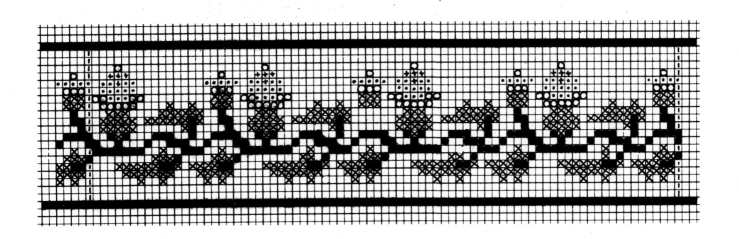

SECTION 10

Monogram Alphabets

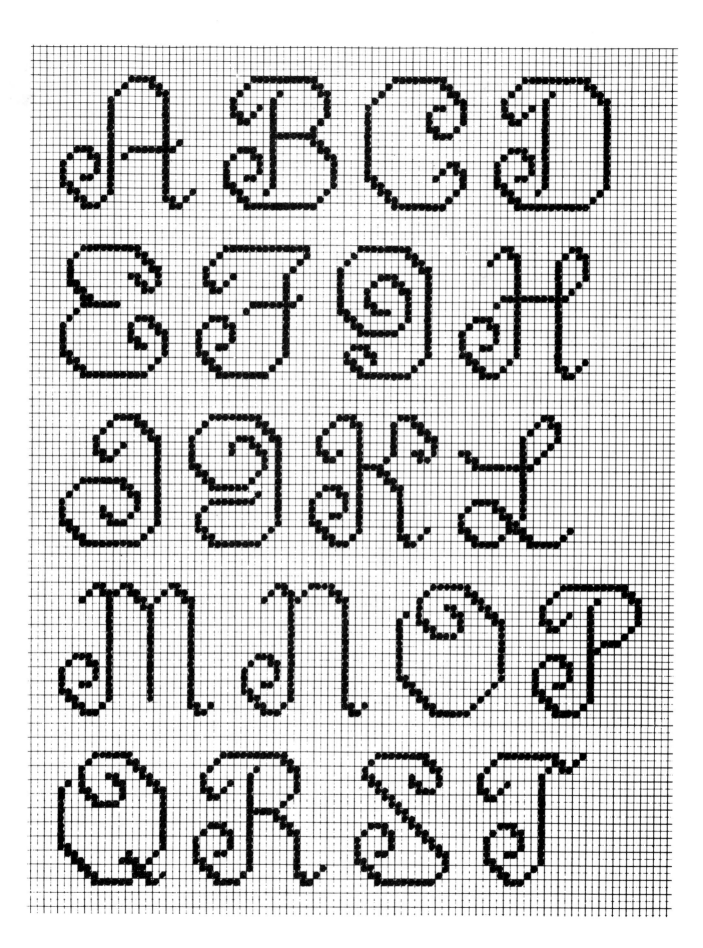

122

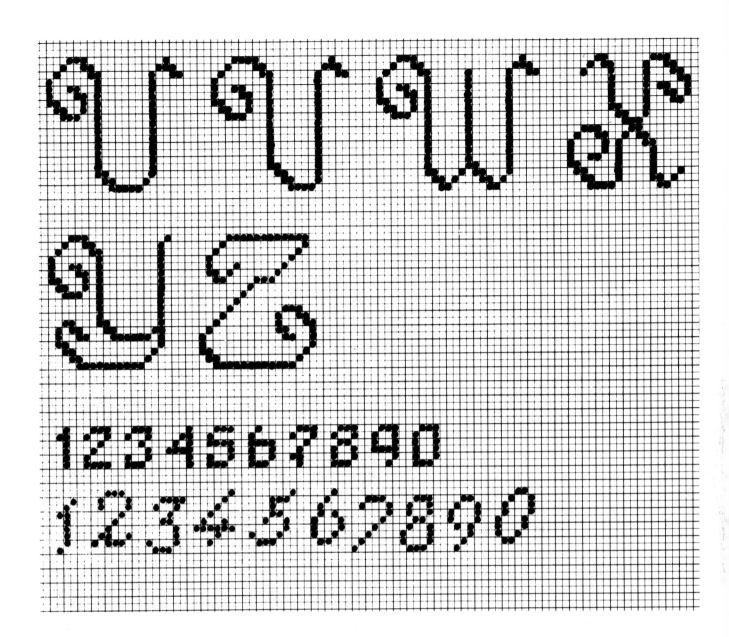

1234567890

1234567890

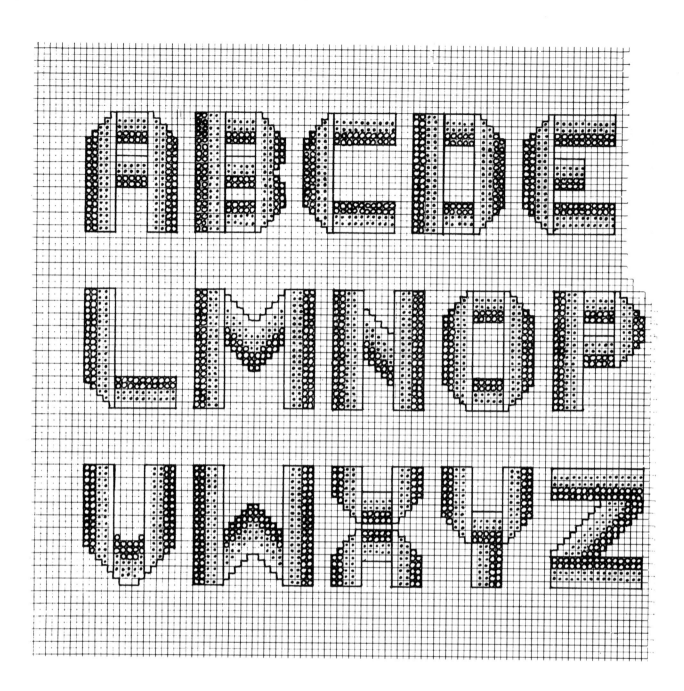

124

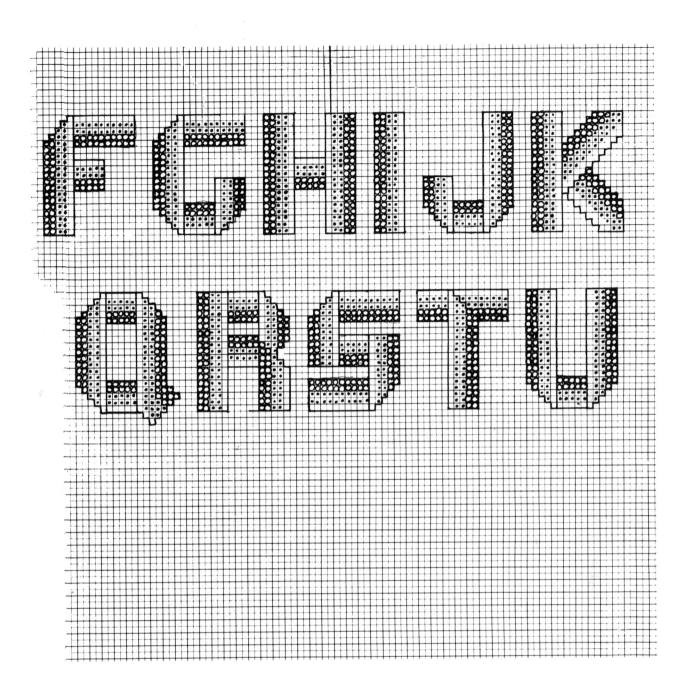

125

SMALL DOTS INDICATE
OPTIONAL EXTENSIONS

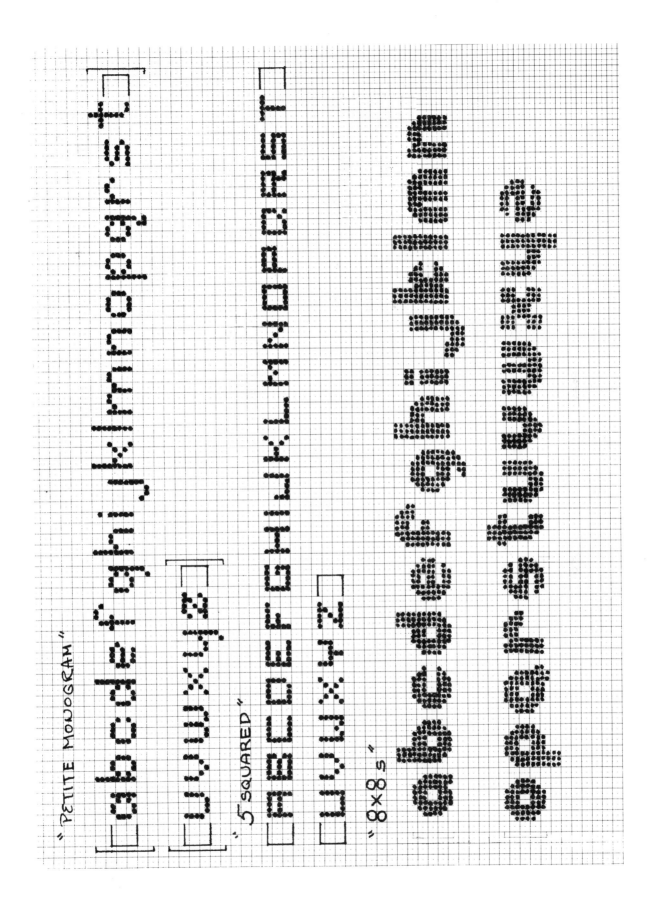

"PETITE MONOGRAM"

abcdefghijklmnopqrst
uvwxyz

"5 SQUARED"

ABCDEFGHIJKLMNOPQRST
UVWXYZ

"8×8's"

Appendix: Resources

In the event that you cannot find the recommended materials locally, you can write to these companies for information and assistance.

Floss and Metallic Threads:

DMC Corporation
107 Trumbull St.
Elizabeth, NJ 07206

Nepo™ and Glad Rags™ Markers:

Sanford Corporation
2740 Washington Blvd.
Bellwood, IL 60104

Belt, Overall, and Suspender Hardware:

E-Z Buckle, Inc.
545 N. Arlington Ave.
East Orange, NJ 07017

Tennis Racquet Cover:

Eagle Buckram Co., Inc.
29 W. 4th St.
New York, NY 10012

Backgammon Frame and Accessories:

Sudberry House
Box 421
Old Lyme, CT 06371

Wooden Accessories:

O. P. Craft Co., Inc.
425 Warren St.
Sandusky, OH 44870
($1.00 charge for catalog)

Christmas Ornaments Booklet— "Designs for Fun" 24 patterns:

Sign of the Bee, Inc.
P.O. Box 5337
St. Louis, MO 63115

Tennis Shoe "Finishing":

Needlepoint Etc.
9785 Clayton Rd.
St. Louis, MO 63124

Index of Designs